THE CAREER COMPASS

I n the modern world, the concept of a traditional career has evolved into a kaleidoscope of possibilities, each as vibrant and unique as the individuals who embark upon them. The once-clear boundaries of professional trajectories have given way to a boundless landscape where passions, skills, and ambitions converge to create a rich mosaic of livelihoods.

This book invites you on a captivating journey through the labyrinth of career choices that define our contemporary age. From the well-trodden avenues of medicine and law to the uncharted territories of digital nomadism and social entrepreneurship, the realm of work has expanded into an expansive canvas. Each brushstroke on this canvas represents an individual's pursuit of purpose, fulfillment, and success.

In the following chapters, we will traverse a terrain that spans industries, cultures, and aspirations. We will meet the audacious souls who dared to defy conventions and tread paths less taken. Through their stories, we will witness the profound impact that a single decision—choosing a career path—can have on shaping one's identity and shaping the world.

As we explore into these narratives, we will come to understand that a career is no longer merely a means of livelihood; it is a medium for self-expression, growth, and contribution. Whether you find yourself drawn to the precision of engineering, the creativity of the arts, the analytical depths of research, or the dynamic world of entrepreneurship, this book seeks to serve as a compass in your quest for a fulfilling and meaningful career.

But this exploration is not solely about the external avenues and opportunities. It also invites introspection. In a world where the traditional nine-to-five mold is just one brushstroke in the grand tapestry of possibilities, how do we define success? What role does passion play in shaping our choices? How do we navigate the delicate balance between financial stability and pursuing our dreams?

Throughout these pages, we will not only celebrate the diversity of career paths but also unveil the common threads that weave them together. Themes of resilience, adaptability, and the pursuit of purpose emerge as guiding stars in this vast cosmos of choices. Whether you are a student on the cusp of decision, a professional contemplating a change, or simply someone curious about the myriad ways humans engage with their work, "The Career Compass" offers insights, inspiration, and guidance.

As we embark on this expedition into the world of career paths, let us embrace the unknown with an open heart and an eager mind. Whether you are gazing out at the vast expanse of career possibilities with excitement or trepidation, know that you are not alone. As you turn the pages of "The Career Compass," may you find the inspiration, insights, and encouragement to boldly traverse the labyrinthine pathways of success and to craft a narrative uniquely your own. Let us celebrate the power of choice, the beauty of diversity, and the unending potential that lies within each of us to create a life that reflects our truest selves.

Beyond Earth's Grasp: The Astronaut's Odyssey

Humanity has always been drawn to the stars, casting our collective gaze upwards with a mixture of wonder and curiosity. Among the myriad dreams that have fueled our exploration of the cosmos, few have captured the imagination as profoundly as the notion of becoming an astronaut. The life of an astronaut is one of adventure, dedication, and unparalleled discovery, as individuals venture beyond Earth's protective embrace to explore the vastness of space. This section delves into the captivating realm of being an astronaut, examining the rigorous training, the challenges of space travel, the scientific contributions, the impact on personal lives, and the enduring allure of reaching for the stars.

The journey to becoming an astronaut is an arduous one, marked by intense physical, mental, and emotional training. The rigorous selection process is designed to identify individuals who possess not only exceptional scientific knowledge and technical skills but also the resilience to face the unknown challenges of space travel. Astronaut candidates undergo rigorous physical training to build strength and endurance, as well as mental simulations to prepare for the isolation and confined living conditions of space missions. Moreover, teamwork and adaptability are honed through collaborative exercises, as astronauts must work closely with international counterparts on the International Space Station (ISS) and other projects. This preparation extends beyond technical skills, fostering a sense of camaraderie and trust among astronauts—a crucial factor for the success of space missions.

Space travel is a unique and demanding endeavor that challenges the boundaries of human endurance and engineering ingenuity. The microgravity environment of space brings about physiological changes in the human body, including muscle atrophy and bone density loss. Astronauts must combat these effects through rigorous exercise routines and specialized equipment. Moreover, the psychological toll of extended isolation and confinement in space cannot be underestimated. The "Overview Effect," a term coined by astronaut Frank White, describes the profound shift in perspective that astronauts experience when they see Earth from space—a perspective that often leads to a heightened awareness of our planet's fragility and interconnectedness. Balancing the awe of witnessing the cosmos with the physical and emotional demands of space travel underscores the unique challenges that astronauts face.

While the challenges of space exploration are substantial, the contributions that astronauts make to science and human knowledge are equally monumental. Space missions have yielded groundbreaking discoveries in fields ranging from medicine to geology. Research conducted in microgravity has led to insights into osteoporosis, muscle degeneration, and immune system functioning, offering potential benefits for healthcare on Earth. Additionally, the study of celestial bodies provides clues about the origins of our solar system and the fundamental forces that govern the universe. The deployment and maintenance of advanced instruments like the Hubble Space Telescope have revolutionized our understanding of the cosmos, capturing images that have ignited public fascination and deepened our exploration of the universe's mysteries.

Behind the awe-inspiring images and groundbreaking research lie personal sacrifices and unique family dynamics. Astronauts often spend extended periods away from their loved ones, missing birthdays, anniversaries, and other important events. The physical separation and communication delays inherent in space missions can strain relationships and challenge familial bonds. Yet, many astronauts and their families view these sacrifices as part of a greater calling, recognizing that their contributions pave the way for future generations to explore and understand the cosmos. The emotional and psychological toll of space travel on families serves as a reminder of the humanity behind the helmets and spacesuits.

In an age characterized by technological advancements and scientific breakthroughs, the allure of becoming an astronaut remains as potent as ever. The dream of space travel encapsulates our innate desire for adventure, discovery, and the pursuit of the unknown. As private space companies join governmental agencies in the race to explore the cosmos, the possibilities for aspiring astronauts are expanding. Whether it's setting foot on Mars, establishing a lunar base, or uncovering the secrets of distant planets, the astronaut's odyssey continues to captivate the hearts and minds of those who yearn to journey beyond our planet's confines.

Becoming an astronaut is a testament to human ingenuity, resilience, and the unwavering spirit of exploration. From the rigorous training to the challenges of space travel, the contributions to science, the sacrifices of personal lives, and the enduring allure of the cosmos, astronauts embody the essence of adventure and discovery. As we look to the future, the role of astronauts in advancing scientific frontiers and rekindling the human spirit of exploration remains paramount. The legacy of those who have traversed the final frontier serves as a reminder that our dreams of reaching the stars are not just fanciful notions, but bold aspirations that push the boundaries of what is possible, both for individuals and for humanity as a whole.

Chasing Greatness: Inside the World of Professional Athletes

The world of professional sports has long captivated our collective imagination, serving as a stage where human potential is pushed to its limits and greatness is achieved through dedication, discipline, and relentless pursuit of perfection. Becoming a professional athlete is a journey that entails not only unparalleled physical prowess but also mental fortitude, resilience, and a deep love for the sport. This section dives into the multifaceted life of a professional athlete, exploring the rigorous training, the mental and emotional challenges, the rewards of success, the impact on personal lives, and the enduring allure of competing on the grandest stages.

Becoming a professional athlete is often the culmination of years of dedication, beginning with a passion that ignites during childhood. Aspiring athletes devote countless hours to honing their skills, pushing their bodies to achieve new heights, and learning the intricacies of their chosen sport. Training regimes are grueling and unforgiving, as athletes strive to build not only strength and speed but also the technical finesse that distinguishes the elite from the competent. Endurance, resilience, and the ability to bounce back from setbacks are traits that are ingrained through rigorous training sessions, pushing athletes to their limits and beyond. The competitive nature of professional sports demands a level of commitment that goes beyond ordinary dedication, requiring unwavering focus and an unrelenting pursuit of improvement.

While physical prowess is undoubtedly central to an athlete's success, the mental and emotional aspects play an equally crucial role. The psychological pressure of performing at a high level, under the scrutinizing eyes of fans, coaches, and sponsors, can be immense. The fear of failure, the weight of expectations, and the ever-present possibility of injury create a complex mental landscape. Athletes must cultivate mental resilience, employing strategies like visualization, mindfulness, and sports psychology to overcome self-doubt and maintain focus. Balancing the intense emotional highs of victory with the lows of defeat, all while navigating the demands of training, competition, and public perception, requires a unique set of coping skills that shape an athlete's character both on and off the field.

Professional athletes often find themselves on a perpetual emotional roller coaster, where success and failure are intertwined in the pursuit of excellence. The euphoria of victory, whether it's crossing the finish line first, scoring a winning goal, or setting a new record, is a sensation that justifies the years of sacrifice and dedication. These moments of triumph become memories that athletes carry with them throughout their lives, representing the tangible reward for their ceaseless efforts. However, the other side of the coin is equally real—the heartache of defeat. Losing a crucial match, missing a critical shot, or falling short of a long-held goal can evoke profound disappointment and self-doubt. Navigating the emotional aftermath of defeat is as much a part of an athlete's journey as the celebrations of victory.

The life of a professional athlete is often consumed by training, competition, and travel, leaving little time for personal pursuits and relationships. The sacrifices demanded by the profession can strain familial bonds, disrupt social lives, and even compromise mental well-being. While the adulation and recognition that come with success are undeniable, the toll on personal lives is a significant challenge that athletes must navigate. Balancing the rigorous demands of training and competition with maintaining personal relationships, pursuing education, and planning for life beyond the playing field requires careful juggling and an unwavering support system.

Despite the trials and tribulations that come with the

life of a professional athlete, the allure of competing on the grandest stages remains irresistible. The quest for excellence, the pursuit of greatness, and the thrill of pushing oneself to achieve the seemingly impossible are forces that continue to draw individuals to the realm of professional sports. Beyond the individual victories and defeats, athletes often become symbols of inspiration and aspiration, motivating others to pursue their dreams and overcome obstacles. The legacy of professional athletes extends beyond their physical accomplishments, reminding us that the pursuit of excellence is a journey worth undertaking.

Being a professional athlete is a path that combines physical prowess, mental strength, and emotional resilience in a quest for excellence. The dedication to training, the mental and emotional challenges, the thrill of victory, and the impact on personal lives collectively shape the complex tapestry of an athlete's life. From the triumphs that solidify their place in history to the sacrifices that underscore their commitment, professional athletes embody the indomitable human spirit, reminding us that the pursuit of greatness is a journey that transcends the boundaries of the sports arena.

From Aspiration to Healing:
The Doctor's Voyage

Being a doctor is more than just a profession; it's a vocation that demands unwavering dedication, profound empathy, and an unrelenting commitment to the well-being of others. A doctor's journey is characterized by years of rigorous education, intensive training, and a continuous pursuit of knowledge. This section explores into the multifaceted world of being a doctor, exploring the arduous path to medical practice, the challenges of patient care, the ethical responsibilities, the personal sacrifices, and the profound impact on both the doctor's life and the lives they touch.

Becoming a doctor is a rigorous and demanding endeavor that begins with a strong academic foundation. Aspiring doctors navigate years of education, mastering the intricacies of anatomy, physiology, pharmacology, and a plethora of medical sciences. Medical school brings not only academic challenges but also emotional and psychological growth as students grapple with the complexities of human health and the ethical implications of their decisions. Rigorous clinical rotations provide hands-on experience, allowing students to bridge theory and practice under the guidance of experienced physicians. The path to becoming a doctor is marked by intellectual rigor, compassion, and the cultivation of a deep sense of responsibility towards patients and society.

While medical knowledge and technical skills are crucial, the heart of being a doctor lies in the art of healing. Doctors are entrusted with the well-being of their patients, often in their most vulnerable moments. The doctor-patient relationship is built on trust, empathy, and effective communication. From diagnosing ailments to providing treatment options and counseling, doctors must skillfully navigate the delicate balance between clinical expertise and compassionate care. Each patient encounter is an opportunity to alleviate suffering, instill hope, and make a tangible difference in someone's life. The ability to truly listen, empathize, and tailor treatments to individual needs is a hallmark of a skilled and compassionate doctor.

The practice of medicine is imbued with ethical considerations that demand doctors to uphold the highest standards of integrity and responsibility. Ethical dilemmas, such as maintaining patient confidentiality, obtaining informed consent, and ensuring equitable care, are integral to a doctor's daily decisions. The principle of "do no harm" guides medical practice, challenging doctors to weigh the potential benefits of treatment against the possible risks. These moral dilemmas extend beyond the clinic to complex issues like end-of-life care, organ transplantation, and resource allocation. A doctor's ethical compass, rooted in both medical guidelines and personal values, guides them through these challenging decisions.

The life of a doctor is characterized by long hours, demanding schedules, and significant personal sacrifices. Doctors often work beyond the typical nine-to-five, dedicating themselves to patient care and staying up-to-date with the latest medical advancements. The demands of the profession can take a toll on personal relationships and work-life balance. However, the rewards are equally profound. The joy of witnessing patients recover, the satisfaction of making accurate diagnoses, and the knowledge that one's expertise has a direct impact on improving lives are sources of deep fulfillment. The doctor's vocation goes beyond financial compensation; it's a calling that brings a sense of purpose and meaning to their lives.

The impact of a doctor's work extends far beyond individual patient interactions. Doctors play a crucial role in public health, preventive medicine, and medical research. Their contributions to medical literature, clinical trials, and public health campaigns shape the trajectory of healthcare and improve the lives of countless individuals. Additionally, doctors inspire future generations of healthcare professionals, passing on their knowledge, values, and dedication. The ripple effect of a doctor's care and guidance touches families, communities, and society at large, creating a legacy that transcends time and individual practice.

Being a doctor is a vocation that intertwines science, compassion, and ethics into a profound journey of healing. From the rigorous education to the challenges of patient care, the ethical responsibilities to the personal sacrifices, the life of a doctor is characterized by a relentless pursuit of excellence and a deep commitment to humanity's well-being. Doctors hold the power to alleviate suffering, instill hope, and guide patients towards better health. Their path is not just a profession; it's a noble calling that shapes lives, transforms communities, and embodies the essence of humanity's compassion and resilience.

Defending Justice: Exploring the Path of a Lawyer

The legal profession stands as a cornerstone of modern society, upholding the principles of justice, equity, and the rule of law. Lawyers play a pivotal role in navigating the complex web of laws, advocating for their clients' rights, and ensuring that the wheels of justice continue to turn. Beyond the courtroom drama portrayed in popular media, being a lawyer is a multifaceted journey that demands a comprehensive understanding of the law, refined communication skills, unwavering ethical standards, and a profound dedication to serving both clients and society. This section adventures into the intricate world of being a lawyer, exploring the path to legal practice, the dynamics of client representation, the ethical responsibilities, the personal challenges, and the enduring impact on the legal system and beyond.

Becoming a lawyer is a journey that entails rigorous education and training. Aspiring lawyers embark on years of academic study, delving into the intricacies of the legal system, constitutional principles, case law, and various areas of law such as criminal, civil, corporate, or environmental law. Law school nurtures critical thinking, legal analysis, and effective communication skills, all of which are essential tools for a lawyer's practice. After graduation, aspiring lawyers typically undergo a period of practical training, such as internships or clerkships, to gain firsthand experience of the legal process. This comprehensive education equips lawyers with the foundation to navigate the complexities of the legal landscape.

At the heart of a lawyer's role lies the responsibility to advocate for their clients. Whether representing individuals, corporations, or public entities, lawyers serve as voices of reason, championing their clients' interests within the boundaries of the law. Lawyers collaborate closely with their clients to understand their unique situations, analyze legal options, and develop strategies for resolving disputes or achieving objectives. Effective communication skills are paramount, enabling lawyers to articulate complex legal concepts to clients, judges, juries, and opposing counsel. The ability to construct persuasive arguments, backed by solid legal research, is pivotal in securing favorable outcomes for clients.

Integrity and ethics form the bedrock of the legal profession. Lawyers are bound by ethical codes that emphasize the duty to provide competent representation while upholding the principles of honesty, confidentiality, and fairness. The attorney-client privilege fosters an environment of trust, allowing clients to confide in their lawyers without fear of disclosure. Balancing the pursuit of justice with the responsibility to their clients requires lawyers to navigate delicate ethical dilemmas, particularly when faced with conflicting interests. Upholding justice and promoting the greater good often demand lawyers to act as not just advocates, but also as gatekeepers of the legal system's integrity.

The life of a lawyer is not without its challenges. Lawyers often work long hours, conducting exhaustive research, drafting complex legal documents, and preparing for court appearances. The demands of the profession can place strain on personal lives, leading to a delicate balance between professional commitments and maintaining personal well-being. The adversarial nature of legal practice also exposes lawyers to emotional and psychological stress, particularly when dealing with contentious cases or intense negotiations. The pressure to provide effective representation while managing personal boundaries can be a formidable challenge.

Beyond individual cases, lawyers contribute to shaping legal precedent and influencing societal norms. Landmark cases can establish legal precedents that guide future legal interpretations, impacting how laws are applied in various contexts. Lawyers also engage in advocacy for social justice, influencing policy reforms, and championing causes that align with their values. By participating in public interest work, pro bono services, and community engagement, lawyers contribute to the evolution of the legal landscape and the betterment of society as a whole.

Being a lawyer encompasses more than just a career—it's a dedication to upholding justice, promoting equity, and safeguarding the rights of individuals and institutions. Lawyers wield their legal expertise to ensure that the principles of fairness and accountability prevail in society. As they navigate the intricate legal landscape, advocate for their clients, uphold ethical standards, and contribute to shaping legal precedents, lawyers continue to be indispensable pillars of a just and equitable society.

Venturing Boldly: Exploring the Entrepreneurial Journey

The realm of entrepreneurship is a vibrant landscape where creativity, determination, and risk-taking converge to shape the course of industries, economies, and societies. Being an entrepreneur is more than just a career choice; it's a mindset, a lifestyle, and a transformative journey that involves seizing opportunities, navigating challenges, and driving change. This section delves into the dynamic world of entrepreneurship, exploring the process of starting and growing a business, the qualities that define successful entrepreneurs, the risks and rewards, the impact on personal and societal levels, and the enduring allure of shaping one's destiny through innovation.

At the heart of entrepreneurship lies the ability to identify gaps in the market, conceive innovative solutions, and transform ideas into viable businesses. Entrepreneurs possess a unique ability to view challenges as opportunities, recognizing unmet needs and devising ways to address them. The inception of a business idea often involves rigorous research, feasibility assessments, and a deep understanding of market dynamics. Entrepreneurs must be perceptive and adaptable, embracing change as a constant and leveraging their insights to create products or services that resonate with their target audience.

Starting a business is merely the first step on an intricate journey of growth and development. Entrepreneurs face multifaceted challenges, including securing funding, building a strong team, developing a scalable business model, and navigating the complexities of regulations and competition. The journey demands resilience, as entrepreneurs must adapt to setbacks, pivot their strategies, and continue evolving their businesses to remain relevant. Effective leadership, strategic decision-making, and the ability to learn from failures are critical traits that successful entrepreneurs cultivate as they shepherd their ventures through various stages of growth.

The entrepreneurial path is not devoid of risk; it involves venturing into the unknown, making calculated decisions with uncertain outcomes, and assuming personal and financial responsibility for the success of the business. Entrepreneurs often invest significant time, effort, and capital into their ventures, with the understanding that failure is a possibility. The risk-reward dynamic shapes the entrepreneurial mindset, motivating individuals to take bold actions, pursue innovative ideas, and push boundaries. The potential for financial gain, creative fulfillment, and the impact on industries and communities make the entrepreneurial journey a compelling and transformative experience.

Being an entrepreneur transcends business; it influences personal lives and societal progress. Entrepreneurs often navigate a delicate balance between their professional aspirations and personal well-being, as the demands of entrepreneurship can be all-encompassing. The entrepreneurial journey also has a profound impact on communities and economies. Successful ventures generate employment opportunities, stimulate economic growth, and contribute to technological advancements. Moreover, entrepreneurs can catalyze social change by addressing pressing challenges, fostering sustainable practices, and championing philanthropic endeavors that have a lasting impact on society.

The allure of entrepreneurship is rooted in the freedom to innovate, disrupt industries, and bring transformative ideas to fruition. The journey's appeal lies in the ability to shape one's destiny, create a legacy, and leave a mark on the world. Entrepreneurs exemplify the spirit of individual agency and the power to challenge conventions, redefine norms, and drive progress. The ever-evolving landscape of technology and globalization continues to provide new opportunities for aspiring entrepreneurs to explore novel business models, leverage emerging trends, and create solutions that address evolving needs.

Being an entrepreneur encapsulates a daring pursuit of innovation, risk-taking, and transformative change. From the inception of an idea to the growth of a business, entrepreneurs navigate a dynamic journey that demands resilience, strategic acumen, and the ability to capitalize on opportunities. The entrepreneurial path shapes not only individual destinies but also influences economies, industries, and societies at large. It embodies the spirit of forging new horizons, embracing challenges, and leaving an indelible legacy through the power of innovation and vision.

Courage Under Fire: Exploring the Life of a Firefighter

The role of a firefighter extends far beyond the iconic image of rushing into burning buildings. It is a vocation rooted in selflessness, courage, and an unwavering commitment to protecting lives, property, and communities. The life of a firefighter is a blend of adrenaline-fueled responses to emergencies, rigorous training, camaraderie, and the emotional toll of witnessing devastation. This section dives into the multifaceted world of being a firefighter, exploring the rigorous training, the challenges of fire and rescue operations, the emotional and physical toll, the bond of brotherhood, and the enduring legacy of those who stand as guardians of the flames.

The journey to becoming a firefighter begins with rigorous training that prepares individuals to respond effectively to a range of emergencies. Training programs encompass fire suppression techniques, search and rescue operations, medical skills, hazardous material handling, and disaster response protocols. Firefighters are trained not only to combat fires but also to address medical emergencies, natural disasters, and other crises that endanger lives. Simulations and hands-on exercises immerse trainees in realistic scenarios, enabling them to develop the physical and mental skills required to make split-second decisions under pressure. This comprehensive training forms the bedrock of a firefighter's capability to serve their community with skill and precision.

Firefighters stand as the first line of defense against the unpredictable and destructive forces of fire. Their response to emergencies is characterized by swift action, coordination, and a commitment to preserving life and property. Whether extinguishing flames, rescuing trapped individuals, providing medical aid, or safeguarding against hazardous materials, firefighters often find themselves facing life-or-death situations that require extraordinary courage and professionalism. The ability to work effectively as a team, communicate clearly amidst chaos, and remain composed in high-stress environments is critical to their success.

The challenges of firefighting extend beyond the immediate dangers of flames and smoke. Firefighters frequently bear witness to traumatic incidents, including loss of life, severe injuries, and property destruction. The emotional toll of responding to these situations can lead to psychological stress, compassion fatigue, and post-traumatic stress disorder (PTSD). The burden of witnessing tragedy while striving to save lives requires emotional resilience and a support system that extends beyond the firehouse. Fire departments increasingly recognize the importance of providing mental health resources and peer support to ensure firefighters can cope with the emotional challenges of their profession.

The fire service fosters a strong sense of camaraderie and brotherhood among firefighters. The shared experiences, intense training, and mutual reliance in life-threatening situations create bonds that extend beyond professional duties. Firefighters function as a tight-knit family, supporting one another on and off the job. This bond is pivotal for maintaining mental well-being, as firefighters can openly share their experiences and seek guidance from peers who understand the unique challenges they face. The sense of unity, mutual respect, and trust within the fire service community underscores the notion that firefighters are not just colleagues but also extended family members.

The legacy of firefighters is defined by their commitment to selfless service and sacrifice. Firefighters put their lives on the line daily to protect their communities, often without seeking recognition or praise. The selflessness of their work is evident in their dedication to safeguarding lives during emergencies and promoting fire prevention and safety education. Beyond their operational duties, firefighters engage with their communities through outreach programs, educational initiatives, and charitable efforts. The legacy of firefighters extends beyond their individual careers, serving as a reminder of the extraordinary courage and compassion that define their calling.

Being a firefighter is a noble calling that embodies the principles of courage, compassion, and unwavering dedication. From rigorous training to responding to emergencies, from emotional resilience to the bonds of brotherhood, firefighters stand as the embodiment of selfless service. They forge their legacy through their willingness to confront danger head-on, their commitment to saving lives, and their enduring impact on the safety and well-being of their communities. The flames they battle symbolize not only the destructive forces they tame but also the enduring spirit of those who choose to be guardians of the flames.

Into the Inferno: Tales from the Frontline of Wildland Firefighting

Amidst the rugged landscapes and towering forests, a unique breed of heroes emerges—the wildland firefighters. This section explores into the captivating world of wildland firefighters, exploring their exceptional role, the skills they harness, the challenges they face, the rewards they embrace, and the profound impact they have on both the environment and communities they protect.

Wildland firefighters are the unsung guardians of our natural spaces, charged with containing and extinguishing fires that threaten forests, grasslands, and wilderness areas. Unlike their urban counterparts, these brave individuals confront wildfires in some of the most remote and challenging terrains. Their mission extends beyond saving property; they are tasked with preserving the delicate balance of ecosystems and safeguarding the homes of countless wildlife species. Wildland firefighters serve as the first line of defense against the ferocity of nature's flames.

The role of a wildland firefighter demands a mastery of skills that bridge physical prowess and strategic thinking. These individuals undergo rigorous training to become proficient in fire behavior, safety protocols, and containment strategies. They wield specialized tools like chainsaws, pulaskis, and drip torches with a finesse that only experience can impart. Their fitness levels are exceptional, as they must carry heavy equipment through challenging terrains while battling extreme weather conditions. Additionally, communication and teamwork are vital, as they coordinate efforts with other firefighters to create firebreaks and control lines.

Wildland firefighters grapple with a multitude of challenges, many of which stem from the unpredictable and uncontrollable nature of wildfires. The physical demands of the job are immense; they endure grueling hours in sweltering heat or freezing cold, often hiking long distances while carrying heavy loads. The ever-changing behavior of fires requires them to make split-second decisions that can influence the trajectory of the blaze. They face the risk of smoke inhalation, falling trees, and shifting winds that can rapidly alter the course of the fire. Yet, despite these challenges, wildland firefighters stand resilient, their commitment unyielding in the face of adversity.

The rewards of being a wildland firefighter extend far beyond monetary compensation. Every fire successfully contained is a testament to their hard work and dedication, a triumph over the destructive forces of nature. The camaraderie formed amongst fellow firefighters creates bonds that last a lifetime, forged through shared challenges and victories. The gratitude expressed by the communities they serve serves as a poignant reminder of the impact they have on people's lives. Moreover, their efforts contribute to the preservation of vital ecosystems, ensuring that future generations can continue to enjoy the beauty and resources of the wilderness.

The impact of wildland firefighters is profound and far-reaching. Their heroic efforts protect lives, property, and the environment, preventing wildfires from spiraling into uncontrolled catastrophes. By managing natural fire cycles, they help ecosystems regenerate and maintain their health. Their work also serves as a powerful reminder of the resilience of the human spirit in the face of nature's fury. Additionally, they play an educational role, raising awareness about fire safety, prevention, and responsible land management. The legacy they leave is one of dedication, sacrifice, and a commitment to preserving the delicate balance between humans and nature.

Wildland firefighters stand as a testament to humanity's ability to confront and conquer the untamed forces of the natural world. Their role is a fusion of courage, skill, and unwavering dedication to preserving both life and land.

Through sweltering heat, biting cold, and challenging terrains, they embody the resilience required to protect our planet's most cherished resources. As they battle the flames, they emerge as unsung heroes, safeguarding not only communities but the very essence of the wild. The legacy of a wildland firefighter is one that burns brightly—an enduring symbol of bravery, unity, and the profound impact of human dedication.

Unveiling the Life of a Law Enforcement Officer

The role of a police officer extends beyond its portrayal in media and popular culture. It is a vocation deeply rooted in the principles of safeguarding communities, enforcing laws, and upholding justice. Being a police officer is a multifaceted journey that demands courage, integrity, and a commitment to public service. This section adventures into the complex world of being a police officer, exploring the path to law enforcement, the challenges of maintaining public safety, the ethical responsibilities, the personal and societal impact, and the enduring importance of fostering positive relationships between law enforcement and the community.

Becoming a police officer is a journey that often begins with a desire to serve one's community and ensure public safety. Aspiring officers typically undergo a rigorous selection process that includes background checks, physical fitness tests, psychological evaluations, and comprehensive training. Law enforcement academies provide essential education on legal procedures, ethics, conflict resolution, community policing, and emergency response tactics. The training is designed to prepare officers for the myriad situations they may encounter while patrolling neighborhoods, investigating crimes, and maintaining order.

A police officer's role extends beyond enforcing laws; it involves engaging with diverse communities and fostering trust. Officers are the first responders to emergencies, mediating disputes, providing assistance to those in need, and ensuring the safety of individuals and neighborhoods. Effective communication skills are pivotal in defusing tense situations and building rapport with the community. Balancing the enforcement of laws with empathy and understanding requires officers to navigate complex ethical and moral dilemmas, making decisions that uphold justice while respecting individual rights.

The life of a police officer is marked by daily challenges that range from routine tasks to high-stress situations. Officers must be prepared to handle emergencies, respond to criminal incidents, and make split-second decisions that can have far-reaching consequences. These decisions are often scrutinized by the public and media, shining a spotlight on the delicate balance between protecting lives and ensuring due process. Public perception of law enforcement can be influenced by isolated incidents, leading to debates about police practices, accountability, and reform. Navigating these challenges demands open communication, transparency, and a commitment to continuous improvement within the law enforcement profession.

The ethical responsibilities of police officers encompass a wide spectrum, from upholding individual rights to demonstrating fairness and impartiality. Officers are entrusted with maintaining the public's trust through their actions, decisions, and interactions. Ethical dilemmas may arise when officers are faced with situations that test their principles, such as witnessing misconduct by colleagues or making difficult choices that may impact their safety or that of others. The ability to uphold ethical standards, even in the face of adversity, is paramount to maintaining the public's confidence in law enforcement.

The impact of a police officer's work transcends individual interactions; it influences the relationships between law enforcement and the community. Community-oriented policing emphasizes collaboration between officers and residents to address local concerns, build trust, and prevent crime. Officers engage in community outreach, educational programs, and partnerships with organizations to foster positive relationships and enhance public safety. By actively involving the community in the decision-making process, officers can better understand the unique challenges faced by different neighborhoods and tailor their approaches to specific needs.

Being a police officer is a profound responsibility that demands courage, integrity, and a dedication to public service. From rigorous training to navigating ethical dilemmas, from maintaining public safety to fostering positive community relationships, police officers stand as guardians of trust within society. The enduring importance of law enforcement in upholding justice and ensuring the safety of communities underscores the significance of fostering mutual respect, empathy, and open dialogue between law enforcement officers and the communities they serve. As society evolves, the role of a police officer remains a vital pillar of public safety and the preservation of social harmony.

Unveiling Truths: The Art and Pursuit of Private Investigation

Private investigators, the modern-day sleuths, embark on a clandestine journey to uncover truths hidden beneath layers of secrecy. With their sharp instincts, analytical minds, and resourceful techniques, they serve as independent agents of justice and information. This section delves into the realm of a private investigator, exploring the significance of their role, the diverse responsibilities they embrace, the skills they master, the challenges they confront, and the sense of purpose they find in unveiling mysteries that lie beyond the surface.

Private investigators play a critical role in various domains, from legal proceedings to personal matters. They assist individuals, law firms, and corporations in gathering evidence, verifying claims, and uncovering hidden information. Private investigators bridge gaps in information that may not be readily available through traditional means, contributing to informed decisions and legal proceedings. Their work has the potential to influence outcomes in legal cases, corporate disputes, and personal affairs.

The responsibilities of a private investigator span a wide spectrum, encompassing investigations into legal, corporate, and personal matters. They conduct background checks, locate missing persons, gather evidence for legal cases, and conduct surveillance operations. Private investigators may also specialize in areas such as insurance fraud investigation, cybersecurity, or digital forensics. Their work involves collecting and analyzing information through interviews, research, and observation, often collaborating with law enforcement and legal professionals.

Being a successful private investigator requires a blend of investigative skills, adaptability, and ethical considerations. Private investigators must possess keen observation skills to detect patterns, body language, and inconsistencies in information. Proficiency in research techniques and access to various databases are essential for gathering relevant information. Additionally, strong communication skills facilitate interactions with clients, witnesses, and potential sources of information. Ethical considerations guide private investigators in conducting legal and unbiased investigations while respecting privacy and confidentiality.

The life of a private investigator is not without its challenges. Working irregular hours, including nights and weekends, is common to capture events as they unfold. Maintaining discretion and confidentiality while conducting investigations can be demanding, as well as managing potentially risky situations during surveillance operations. Moreover, the uncertainty of outcomes and the weight of uncovering sensitive information can have emotional and psychological implications. However, the rewards are substantial. The satisfaction of solving complex cases, reuniting families, providing closure, and contributing to justice and truth makes being a private investigator an inherently fulfilling career.

In conclusion, being a private investigator is a dynamic journey that combines intuition, research, and analytical thinking. Private investigators serve as seekers of truth, offering their expertise to uncover hidden facts and unravel mysteries. Their significance extends beyond the realm of investigations; they contribute to justice, fairness, and resolution. Despite the challenges, the rewards of providing closure, restoring peace of mind, and contributing to legal proceedings create a sense of purpose that resonates deeply. Private investigators are the envoys of truth, embodying the pursuit of answers that lie beneath the surface, one investigation at a time.

Stepping into Character: Exploring the Craft of an Actor

Being an actor is an intricate dance between reality and imagination, where individuals bring characters to life and transport audiences to different worlds. Beyond the glamour of red carpets and the allure of fame, the life of an actor is marked by dedication, vulnerability, and a relentless pursuit of artistic excellence. This section dives into the captivating realm of being an actor, exploring the process of embodying diverse roles, the challenges of the profession, the emotional and creative demands, the impact on personal lives, and the enduring allure of storytelling through performance.

At the heart of acting lies the art of transformation —stepping into the shoes of characters that span various eras, personalities, and emotions. Actors immerse themselves in research, studying scripts, historical contexts, and psychological nuances to fully understand their roles. The process involves channeling emotions, adapting physicality, and mastering accents or dialects, all while infusing their own interpretations to create a unique portrayal. This metamorphosis requires a deep connection with the character's motivations, desires, and conflicts, enabling actors to deliver performances that resonate authentically with audiences.

The life of an actor is not without its challenges. The pursuit of roles can be competitive and unpredictable, leading to periods of uncertainty and self-doubt. Auditions, rejections, and the need to continually prove oneself can take a toll on an actor's confidence. The demanding schedules of rehearsals, filming, and performances often result in irregular hours and tight timelines, leaving little room for personal life or relaxation. Moreover, the ability to portray a range of emotions authentically requires tapping into deep emotional reservoirs, sometimes leading to emotional exhaustion. The path of an actor demands tenacity, resilience, and a strong support system to navigate these challenges.

Acting is not just about memorizing lines and hitting marks; it involves baring one's soul to evoke genuine emotions in the audience. Actors must harness their own emotional experiences, empathize with characters, and convey a spectrum of feelings—from joy to sorrow, anger to love— with authenticity. This emotional vulnerability requires a deep introspective journey, as actors delve into their own psyches to tap into universal human experiences. The ability to empathize with characters and translate those emotions onto the stage or screen is a testament to the power of acting as a medium for connection and catharsis.

The life of an actor often demands a delicate balance between personal aspirations and professional commitments. Irregular schedules, long hours, and the need for constant self-improvement can strain personal relationships and impede work-life balance. The transient nature of the profession, with actors often moving from one project to another, can disrupt stability and personal routines. While fame and recognition are alluring aspects, they come with a price—privacy intrusion, public scrutiny, and the pressure to maintain an image. Navigating personal aspirations, relationships, and artistic pursuits is an ongoing challenge for actors seeking fulfillment both on and off the stage.

Despite the challenges, the allure of acting remains unyielding. The stage and screen offer actors a platform to communicate stories, challenge perspectives, and provoke emotions on a profound level. The ability to transport audiences to different worlds, evoke laughter and tears, and elicit introspection through performance is a privilege that few other professions provide. Actors have the unique opportunity to contribute to cultural narratives, advocate for social change, and leave a lasting impact through their artistry. The enduring magic of storytelling and the thrill of embodying diverse characters continue to draw individuals into the captivating world of acting.

Being an actor is a journey that encompasses creativity, vulnerability, and a deep connection to the human experience. From embodying characters to navigating challenges, from expressing emotions authentically to balancing personal and professional lives, actors bring stories to life in a way that resonates with audiences across cultures and generations. The art of acting captures the essence of humanity, offering a mirror through which society reflects upon itself. As thespians step onto stages and screens, they play an essential role in shaping culture, provoking thought, and reminding us of the profound impact of storytelling on the human soul.

Harmonizing Passions: Embarking
on the Path of a Musician

The life of a musician is a symphony of passion, creativity, and relentless dedication to the art of sound. Beyond the enchanting performances on stage and the harmonious melodies that captivate audiences, being a musician is a journey marked by rigorous training, unwavering commitment, and the profound impact of artistic expression. This section explores into the multifaceted realm of being a musician, exploring the process of honing musical skills, the challenges of artistic pursuit, the emotional and intellectual demands, the transformative power of music, and the enduring allure of crafting melodies that resonate across cultures and generations.

Becoming a musician entails a rigorous journey of learning and mastering a chosen instrument or vocal technique. Musicians invest countless hours in practice, refining techniques, scales, and musical theories to achieve precision and fluency. The pursuit of excellence requires not only technical skill but also a deep understanding of musicality, interpretation, and dynamics. Whether a soloist or a member of an ensemble, musicians collaborate to create harmonious performances that capture the essence of the composer's vision while infusing their unique interpretation.

The life of a musician is filled with both artistic rewards and challenges. Musicians often face the pressure to continually evolve their skills, adapt to different genres, and explore new avenues of musical expression. The competitive nature of the industry demands perseverance and resilience in the face of auditions, rejections, and the pursuit of opportunities. The unpredictability of gig-based work and the quest for financial stability can create uncertainty. Yet, these challenges are met with a passion that fuels musicians to keep learning, experimenting, and refining their craft.

Music is a universal language that transcends words, communicating emotions, stories, and experiences that touch the human soul. Musicians bear the responsibility of conveying emotions through their performances, tapping into their own experiences and empathy to connect with audiences. This emotional connection requires vulnerability, courage, and the ability to harness personal emotions to amplify the impact of a composition. Beyond emotions, musicians also engage intellectually, deciphering complex musical scores, exploring historical contexts, and making interpretative choices that breathe life into compositions.

Music holds a transformative power that extends beyond entertainment—it can evoke emotions, inspire change, and provide solace in times of joy or sorrow. Musicians contribute to the cultural fabric of society, channeling their creativity to reflect contemporary issues, convey historical narratives, or convey personal experiences. Music can foster cross-cultural understanding, transcend language barriers, and unite people through shared emotional experiences. Musicians often use their platform to advocate for social causes, lending their voices to amplify messages of unity, peace, and progress.

The allure of being a musician lies in the ability to create timeless art that resonates across generations. Whether performing classical symphonies, contemporary pop hits, or experimental compositions, musicians contribute to a rich tapestry of human expression. Music has the capacity to transport listeners to different times, cultures, and emotional landscapes, leaving an indelible mark on the collective memory of humanity. Musicians continue to draw inspiration from the past while shaping the future, as they compose, perform, and share their passion with audiences worldwide.

Being a musician is a journey of creative expression, emotional connection, and unwavering dedication to the art of sound. Musicians craft melodies that bridge cultures, convey emotions, and ignite imagination. From mastering instruments to navigating artistic challenges, from evoking emotions to advocating for change, musicians shape the world through their compositions and performances. As they continue to explore new horizons, embrace diverse genres, and channel their creativity into their work, musicians play an instrumental role in shaping the rhythm of humanity's shared narrative.

Ink and Imagination: Navigating
the Path of an Author

Being an author is a journey of imagination, creativity, and the profound impact of words. Beyond the pages of books and the allure of storytelling, the life of an author is marked by dedication, introspection, and an unwavering commitment to the craft of writing. This section adventures into the intricate realm of being an author, exploring the process of crafting narratives, the challenges of the writing journey, the emotional and intellectual demands, the connection between authors and readers, and the enduring allure of leaving a literary legacy.

At the core of being an author lies the art of weaving narratives that transport readers to different worlds, eras, and perspectives. Authors are the architects of stories, meticulously crafting characters, settings, and plots that engage the imagination. The process begins with inspiration—a spark of an idea that gradually unfolds into a complex tapestry of words. Authors invest time in research, character development, and world-building, ensuring that their narratives resonate authentically with readers. The ability to create vivid scenes, evoke emotions, and spark reflection is the hallmark of a skilled author.

The life of an author is a journey paved with both artistic rewards and challenges. The act of writing demands discipline, dedication, and resilience in the face of self-doubt and creative blocks. Authors often experience the ebb and flow of motivation, navigating the highs of creative breakthroughs and the lows of wrestling with writer's block. The revision process is equally crucial, requiring authors to refine their work, seek feedback, and fine-tune their narratives. The pursuit of publication can be competitive, with authors navigating the complexities of query letters, literary agents, and publishing houses.

Writing is an intimate process that demands emotional

vulnerability and intellectual rigor. Authors draw from their personal experiences, emotions, and perspectives to infuse authenticity into their work. Creating relatable characters and authentic dialogue involves tapping into human emotions and empathy. The intellectual demands encompass meticulous research, ensuring accuracy in historical details, scientific concepts, or cultural nuances. Authors blend creativity with intellect, using words to convey complex ideas, spark conversations, and resonate with readers on profound levels.

The relationship between authors and readers is a unique and symbiotic one. Authors create narratives with the intention of evoking emotions, sparking reflection, and fostering connections. Readers, in turn, engage with these narratives, finding solace, inspiration, and new perspectives within the pages. The act of reading becomes a shared experience between authors and readers, transcending time and distance. Authors have the power to shape readers' worldviews, challenge assumptions, and offer insights into the human condition through their narratives.

The allure of being an author is grounded in the ability to leave a lasting literary legacy. Through their words, authors contribute to the cultural fabric of society, reflecting contemporary issues, preserving historical narratives, and exploring the depths of human emotion. Literary works endure across generations, shaping collective memory and influencing cultural discourse. Authors' stories live on, inspiring future writers, connecting generations, and contributing to the continuous evolution of human expression.

Being an author is a profound journey of creativity, introspection, and connection. From crafting narratives to navigating challenges, from evoking emotions to leaving a lasting legacy, authors have the power to shape minds, stir hearts, and ignite imagination. As they continue to explore diverse genres, challenge conventions, and share their unique perspectives, authors play a pivotal role in the ongoing tapestry of human expression. Through their words, they transcend time, space, and cultural boundaries, leaving behind echoes of imagination that resonate through the corridors of literature and into the hearts of readers.

Guiding Minds: Navigating the
Pathways of Education as a Teacher

Education is the cornerstone of progress, and at its heart lies the pivotal role of a teacher. A teacher's impact extends far beyond the classroom, shaping not only the minds of students but also the future of society. The responsibility of nurturing young minds and cultivating a passion for learning is a privilege that comes with significant challenges and rewards. This section delves into the multifaceted nature of being a teacher, highlighting the importance of their role, the qualities that define an exceptional educator, the challenges they face, and the lasting impact they leave on their students.

Teachers are the architects of knowledge, constructing the foundation upon which students build their dreams and aspirations. They hold the power to ignite curiosity and kindle the flame of lifelong learning. In a rapidly evolving world, teachers serve as beacons of wisdom, helping students navigate through a sea of information. Beyond academic subjects, teachers impart life skills, moral values, and critical thinking abilities, equipping students to thrive in a complex society. Through their guidance, teachers empower the next generation with the tools to become active and responsible citizens, driving progress and positive change.

Exceptional teachers possess a unique blend of qualities that set them apart. Firstly, they exhibit unwavering dedication to their students' growth. This dedication fuels a genuine passion for teaching, inspiring students to embrace learning with enthusiasm. Effective communication skills are another hallmark of great teachers, enabling them to convey complex ideas in ways that resonate with diverse learning styles. Patience and empathy are essential virtues, as they allow teachers to understand and support students facing various challenges. Furthermore, adaptability is crucial, given the evolving nature of education and the need to incorporate innovative teaching methods. Lastly, a sense of creativity transforms ordinary lessons into engaging and memorable experiences, fostering a deep love for learning.

The journey of a teacher is not without obstacles. One significant challenge is the increasing diversity of classrooms, where teachers encounter students from various cultural backgrounds, learning abilities, and socioeconomic statuses. Addressing the individual needs of each student while maintaining a cohesive learning environment demands remarkable skill and resourcefulness. Additionally, the education landscape is influenced by technological advancements that demand teachers to integrate digital tools effectively. The workload, too, can be overwhelming, with lesson planning, grading, and administrative tasks consuming substantial time and energy. Despite these challenges, dedicated teachers find ways to overcome them, driven by their commitment to their students' success.

The influence of a teacher reverberates long after students leave the classroom. Teachers leave an indelible mark on their students' lives, instilling values, igniting passions, and fostering confidence. Many successful individuals attribute their achievements to the guidance of a mentor who believed in their potential. Moreover, the cumulative effect of exceptional teachers is felt throughout society. The doctors, engineers, artists, and leaders who shape our world often credit their successes to the educators who nurtured their talents. As these students grow into adults, they carry forward the values and knowledge imparted by their teachers, shaping a more informed and compassionate society.

Being a teacher is a vocation that holds immense power. It is a journey of dedication, resilience, and unwavering commitment to shaping the minds of the future. Through their passion, adaptability, and empathy, teachers become architects of change, sculpting a better world one student at a time. As we celebrate the profound impact of teachers, it is essential to recognize that their work extends far beyond the classroom, transcending generations and leaving an enduring legacy. Just as education is a beacon of enlightenment, teachers illuminate the path to a brighter future for all of humanity.

Brushstrokes of Creativity:
Navigating the Canvas of
an Artistic Journey

Being an artist is a unique and transformative journey that requires passion, creativity, resilience, and a deep connection with one's inner self. Artists are the architects of imagination, crafting the intangible into tangible expressions that resonate with emotions, thoughts, and experiences. This section dives into the multifaceted aspects of being an artist, exploring the reasons individuals embark on this path, the creative process, the challenges they face, and the profound fulfillment that comes from sharing their art with the world.

At the heart of being an artist lies an intrinsic drive fueled by a profound passion for self-expression and creativity. Artists are driven to communicate their thoughts, feelings, and ideas in ways that words often fail to capture. This compulsion to create is often rooted in an individual's unique perspective of the world, as well as their desire to leave a mark on society. The art world is a diverse ecosystem encompassing painters, writers, musicians, actors, and creators of all kinds, each embracing their chosen medium to articulate their innermost visions. For many, being an artist is not merely a career choice, but a calling that demands devotion, as the act of creating becomes intertwined with their very identity.

The creative process is the lifeblood of an artist's journey, a delicate dance between inspiration, experimentation, and refinement. This journey often begins with a spark of inspiration – a fleeting thought, an emotion, or an observation – that ignites the artist's imagination. From there, the process evolves, with artists experimenting with various techniques, styles, and mediums to translate their vision into reality. While some moments are marked by fluidity and flow, creative blocks and self-doubt are equally commonplace. Overcoming these hurdles requires persistence and a willingness to embrace the uncertainty that accompanies the pursuit of originality. Through this process, artists uncover not only their own capabilities but also an evolving sense of who they are as creators.

The path of an artist is not without its challenges. The creative realm can be isolating, demanding long hours of solitary work that tests an artist's resolve. Financial instability is another hurdle, as many artists grapple with inconsistent income streams and the pressure to monetize their creations. The art world's subjectivity can also lead to self-doubt, as artists navigate critiques, rejection, and the constant pursuit of validation. However, it is often these very challenges that fuel an artist's growth and resilience. The struggle against adversity fosters a determination to push boundaries, seek unconventional solutions, and persist in the face of obstacles. The artist's journey becomes a testament to the power of passion and perseverance.

The ultimate reward of being an artist lies in the act of sharing one's creations with the world. Art has the remarkable ability to bridge gaps, spark conversations, and evoke emotions in ways that words alone cannot. When an artist's work resonates with others, a profound connection is forged, transcending boundaries of culture, language, and background. This interaction between artist and audience completes the creative cycle, as the artist's intention meets the viewer's interpretation, giving rise to new perspectives and meanings. The fulfillment derived from touching lives, inspiring change, and leaving a lasting impact is unparalleled, affirming the artist's purpose and validating the arduous journey undertaken.

In conclusion, being an artist is a transformative odyssey defined by passion, creativity, challenges, and fulfillment. Artists are the dreamweavers, transforming the intangible into tangible masterpieces that captivate hearts and minds. The creative process, though riddled with uncertainty and obstacles, becomes a playground for exploration and growth, while the challenges encountered foster resilience and innovation. At the heart of an artist's journey lies the profound reward of sharing their creations, forging connections that transcend time and space. Being an artist is not merely a vocation; it is a way of life that breathes vitality into the mundane and enriches the human experience.

Crafting Culinary Excellence:
Embarking on the Journey of a Chef

Being a chef is a multifaceted and exhilarating journey that transcends the mere act of cooking. It entails mastering the art of flavor, texture, and presentation while embracing innovation and tradition. This section explores into the captivating realm of being a chef, elucidating the passion that drives individuals to pursue this profession, the creative process behind culinary masterpieces, the challenges faced in the kitchen, and the profound satisfaction of delighting palates and forging connections through food.

Becoming a chef is often born out of an unyielding passion for food and a desire to transform it into an art form. Chefs are not only cooks but also creators who curate experiences through gastronomy. This passion is frequently ignited in childhood, where fond memories of family gatherings, delectable aromas, and shared meals lay the foundation for a lifelong love affair with food. The culinary world is a tapestry of cultures, techniques, and ingredients that beckon aspiring chefs to explore, innovate, and push the boundaries of their culinary repertoire. To be a chef is to embrace the role of both scientist and artist, using a palette of flavors to craft dishes that tell stories and evoke emotions.

The creative process in the culinary world is a symphony of innovation, experimentation, and tradition. Chefs are akin to composers, blending ingredients and techniques to create harmonious dishes that tantalize the senses. It begins with the selection of ingredients, a dance between quality, seasonality, and sustainability. Chefs draw inspiration from diverse sources – nature, culture, memories – and translate these inspirations onto the plate. This process demands technical prowess, as well as an acute understanding of how flavors and textures interact. Chefs master the balance between tradition and modernity, finding new ways to reinterpret classic dishes while preserving the essence of their heritage. The kitchen becomes a laboratory, and each plate a canvas, as chefs push the boundaries of culinary imagination.

Behind the scenes, the kitchen is a dynamic and demanding environment that tests a chef's mettle. Long hours, intense pressure, and the need for split-second decisions characterize this space. The kitchen demands precision, coordination, and adaptability, akin to a well-choreographed dance where every movement is deliberate and synchronized. Communication is paramount, as a harmonious kitchen relies on the synergy between chefs, sous-chefs, and kitchen staff. The stress can be overwhelming, yet it is in this crucible that chefs refine their skills, learn to think on their feet, and develop a profound respect for the culinary craft. The heat of the kitchen is where resilience is forged, and a chef's true capabilities are unveiled.

The ultimate fulfillment for a chef lies in the joy of nourishing and delighting others through their creations. Food is a universal language that transcends cultural barriers, enabling chefs to connect with people from all walks of life. The act of sharing a meal fosters a sense of camaraderie, sparking conversations and forging bonds. For a chef, witnessing the pleasure that their dishes bring to diners is a reward beyond measure. This connection extends beyond the plate, as chefs become influencers in promoting sustainable practices, supporting local farmers, and advocating for responsible sourcing. The kitchen becomes a platform for both culinary artistry and social responsibility.

In conclusion, being a chef is a captivating journey that melds passion, creativity, challenge, and fulfillment into a symphony of flavors and experiences. It involves channeling a deep-rooted love for food into a profession that marries tradition and innovation. The creative process transforms ingredients into culinary masterpieces, showcasing the chef's artistic prowess. The kitchen, despite its intensity, is a space of growth, where resilience and expertise are cultivated. Ultimately, the chef's true reward lies in the connections forged through their creations, in the joy of nourishing both body and soul. To be a chef is to be a curator of culture, a storyteller through food, and a catalyst for shared moments of delight and connection.

Taking Flight: Embarking
on the Skies as a Pilot

Being a pilot is more than a profession; it is an embodiment of dreams, courage, and a unique connection with the skies. Pilots are entrusted with the safety of passengers and the mastery of complex machines that defy gravity. This section adventures into the captivating world of being a pilot, exploring the motivation behind choosing this career, the rigorous training and skill development required, the challenges faced both in the cockpit and beyond, and the exhilarating sense of freedom and responsibility that comes with piloting aircraft.

Becoming a pilot often stems from an innate fascination with aviation, a desire to explore the vast expanse of the skies, and the allure of commanding aircraft through different altitudes and destinations. The magic of flight captures the imagination early in life, as many aspiring pilots find themselves gazing up at passing airplanes with a mixture of wonder and longing. For some, this passion is rooted in family traditions or inspirational stories of pioneers who pushed the boundaries of human achievement. The aviation industry offers a diverse range of career paths, from commercial airline pilots to military aviators and private charter pilots, each with its own unique set of challenges and rewards. Becoming a pilot means embracing the thrill of discovery and adventure, balanced with the responsibility of ensuring the safety and well-being of all on board.

The path to becoming a pilot is marked by rigorous training, extensive study, and the acquisition of a diverse skill set. Aspiring pilots must complete comprehensive ground school courses to learn the principles of aerodynamics, aviation regulations, navigation, and meteorology. These theoretical foundations provide the groundwork for practical flight training, during which candidates gain hands-on experience under the guidance of certified flight instructors. Learning to manipulate the controls, manage emergencies, and navigate complex airspace requires precision, focus, and a deep understanding of the aircraft's systems. Hours of flight time, simulated scenarios, and written exams test a pilot's knowledge and adaptability. The training process is a transformative journey that instills discipline, confidence, and a lifelong commitment to safety.

Piloting is not without its challenges, both technical and personal. In the cockpit, pilots must manage a multitude of variables – from weather changes and air traffic control instructions to technical malfunctions – all while ensuring a smooth and safe flight for passengers. The pressure of making split-second decisions and maintaining calm under stress is a constant demand. Moreover, pilots often contend with irregular schedules, long periods away from home, and the physical toll of crossing time zones. Balancing personal life with the demands of the profession requires adaptability and resilience. Additionally, with the aviation industry's ever-evolving landscape, staying updated on new technologies, regulations, and safety protocols is an ongoing commitment.

Despite the challenges, being a pilot offers an unparalleled sense of freedom and responsibility. The ability to navigate the skies, witness breathtaking sunrises and sunsets from above the clouds, and travel to diverse destinations is a privilege unique to this profession. The cockpit becomes a sanctuary of solitude and reflection, where pilots find solace amidst the endless expanse. Alongside this freedom, pilots bear the immense responsibility of the lives entrusted to their care. Safety protocols, meticulous pre-flight checks, and adherence to regulations are paramount. Every flight is a testament to the pilot's expertise and dedication to ensuring the well-being of passengers and crew. The sense of accomplishment that comes from completing a successful flight is deeply gratifying, making the challenges encountered along the way worthwhile.

In conclusion, being a pilot is a remarkable journey that encompasses passion, skill, resilience, and an unbreakable bond with the skies. It is a career that allows individuals to transform childhood dreams into reality, navigating through challenges and uncertainties with a strong commitment to safety. The process of mastering the art of flight is both demanding and rewarding, cultivating expertise and discipline. The pilot's role extends beyond the cockpit, touching the lives of passengers and inspiring a sense of wonder. Ultimately, being a pilot is not just a job; it is an embodiment of freedom, responsibility, and the power to turn aspirations into achievements, while soaring to new heights both personally and professionally.

Cultivating Life: Nurturing the Land and Harvesting Dreams as a Farmer

Being a farmer is a profound vocation that connects individuals to the very essence of life – the land and its cycles. Farmers are stewards of the earth, sowing seeds of sustenance, nurturing growth, and reaping the fruits of their labor. This section delves into the intricate world of being a farmer, exploring the motivations that drive people to choose this calling, the art and science of agriculture, the challenges faced in cultivating the land, and the deep sense of fulfillment derived from fostering a harmonious relationship with nature.

Becoming a farmer often emerges from a deep-rooted love for the land and a desire to contribute to the sustenance of communities. The connection between humans and agriculture spans millennia, with the act of cultivating crops and rearing animals forming the bedrock of civilization. Many farmers inherit their trade through generations, carrying forward age-old traditions and wisdom passed down from their ancestors. For others, a fascination with the intricate balance between nature's rhythms and the science of agriculture becomes the driving force. Regardless of the path, the farming journey is one that requires dedication, resilience, and a profound respect for the earth's generosity.

Farming is a delicate dance between science, intuition, and artistry. Farmers must possess a comprehensive understanding of soil health, weather patterns, pest management, and crop rotations. They must balance these scientific principles with an intimate knowledge of their specific region's microclimate and ecological nuances. The art of agriculture emerges in the decisions made – choosing the right crops for the right season, determining planting depths, and crafting irrigation systems that mimic nature's patterns. This symphony of science and art unfolds in every acre tilled and every seed sown, as farmers orchestrate a harmonious relationship between the land's resources and their goals of sustenance and abundance.

Farming is a journey fraught with challenges, where the unpredictability of nature keeps farmers on their toes. Adverse weather conditions, pests, diseases, and market fluctuations are just a few of the obstacles that can disrupt carefully laid plans. These challenges demand resilience, adaptability, and a proactive approach. Farmers must be quick to adjust strategies, implement sustainable practices, and embrace innovative technologies to safeguard their livelihoods. The unpredictability of farming, while daunting, also fosters a deep connection with the land and a heightened appreciation for the cycles of growth and renewal that characterize agriculture.

The ultimate reward for a farmer lies in the bountiful harvest, the culmination of months of hard work, patience, and unwavering dedication. The act of reaping what has been sown – whether it be crops, fruits, or livestock – carries a sense of accomplishment that transcends words. Every harvested yield becomes a testament to the farmer's stewardship of the land and a testament to the intricate dance between human effort and the earth's generosity. The satisfaction of knowing that the fruits of one's labor nourish communities and contribute to the broader fabric of society is immeasurable.

Beyond the tangible rewards, being a farmer fosters a profound bond with nature, allowing individuals to witness the interconnectedness of all life forms. Farmers are not just producers; they are observers, interpreters, and participants in the intricate web of ecosystems. This connection lends a sense of purpose and humility, as they learn to work with nature's rhythms rather than against them. Farming becomes a way of life that encompasses a reverence for the land, an understanding of the cycles of growth and decay, and a commitment to leaving the earth healthier and more vibrant for future generations.

In conclusion, being a farmer is a revered journey that intertwines science, art, stewardship, and a profound connection with the land. It is a calling that demands dedication, resilience, and a deep respect for the cycles of nature. The act of cultivating the earth and nurturing life is an endeavor that nourishes both body and soul. As farmers cultivate the land, they also cultivate a way of life that is intimately intertwined with the natural world – a testament to the enduring relationship between humanity and the earth's abundant gifts.

Blueprints of Creativity: Unveiling the Journey of an Architect

Being an architect is a distinctive and transformative journey that melds creativity, innovation, and technical expertise. Architects are the visionaries behind the structures that shape our world, crafting spaces that harmonize function and aesthetics. This section dives into the captivating realm of being an architect, exploring the motivations that drive individuals to pursue this profession, the dynamic process of architectural design, the challenges architects encounter, and the immense satisfaction derived from seeing their visions materialize into built environments.

Becoming an architect is often rooted in a fascination with the built environment, a desire to mold spaces that inspire, and a profound appreciation for the interaction between design and human experience. Architects hold the power to shape the world around us, influencing how we live, work, and interact. The spark of architectural inspiration can ignite through diverse sources – from iconic structures that leave a lasting impact to the desire to address societal challenges through design innovation. Architecture is an amalgamation of artistry and engineering, and architects wield a unique blend of creativity and technical prowess to transform abstract concepts into concrete realities.

The process of architectural design is a dynamic journey marked by creativity, collaboration, and the synthesis of numerous elements. Architects are storytellers, weaving narratives through space, form, materiality, and light. Design begins with conceptualization, where architects gather inspiration from various sources – nature, culture, history – and distill them into cohesive ideas. As the design evolves, the architect balances aesthetic considerations with functional requirements, translating visions into feasible plans.

Collaborating with engineers, urban planners, and other stakeholders, architects refine their designs, making intricate decisions that influence everything from structural integrity to energy efficiency. The process is iterative, requiring adaptability and a keen eye for detail.

The path of an architect is not without its challenges. Designing structures that adhere to safety standards, regulations, and budget constraints demands a delicate equilibrium between creativity and practicality. Architects must also grapple with the responsibility of creating spaces that are accessible, sustainable, and responsive to evolving societal needs. Balancing the client's aspirations with the practicalities of construction can sometimes lead to tensions, requiring architects to exercise diplomacy and communication skills. Moreover, overseeing the execution of a design, ensuring its faithful translation from concept to reality, is a demanding task that calls for on-site problem-solving and the ability to adapt to unexpected challenges.

The culmination of an architect's efforts lies in witnessing their designs take shape in the physical world. The satisfaction of watching a building rise from the ground, from the pouring of foundations to the installation of intricate details, is deeply rewarding. Architects experience a profound sense of accomplishment as they see their visions come to life, contributing to the urban fabric and leaving a lasting imprint on communities. This tangible manifestation of creativity underscores the significance of architecture as a discipline that shapes our environment and influences our lives in ways both subtle and profound.

Beyond the aesthetic and functional dimensions, being an architect also entails a responsibility to drive positive change through design. Architects have the unique ability to shape spaces that foster inclusivity, environmental sustainability, and community engagement. From designing energy-efficient buildings to revitalizing neglected urban areas, architects have the power to contribute to the betterment of society. This role as agents of change underscores the ethical dimension of the profession, emphasizing the importance of considering the social, cultural, and environmental impact of architectural interventions.

In conclusion, being an architect is a captivating journey that marries creativity, technical expertise, and a deep appreciation for the built environment. Architects are the sculptors of our surroundings, crafting spaces that inspire, innovate, and reflect the complexities of human life. The process of architectural design is a dynamic tapestry that weaves together aesthetics, functionality, and human experience. Challenges encountered along the way are met with resilience, adaptability, and the commitment to balancing the diverse demands of design. Ultimately, architects find fulfillment in the tangible realization of their visions, seeing their designs enrich communities and leaving a legacy that endures through time. As architects shape the world, they also shape the narratives of our lives, underscoring the profound impact of their craft.

Healing Paws and Hearts: A Journey into Veterinary Care

Veterinarians, the dedicated caretakers of our animal companions, occupy a role that melds compassion, expertise, and medical prowess. With a mission to ensure the health and well-being of animals, they stand as advocates for those who cannot speak for themselves. This section explores into the world of a veterinarian, exploring the significance of their role, the diverse responsibilities they shoulder, the skills they hone, the challenges they face, and the profound sense of purpose that comes from preserving the lives and happiness of animals.

Veterinarians serve as guardians of animal health, playing an essential role in the interconnected web of human-animal relationships. They extend their expertise beyond the realms of medical care, impacting public health through disease prevention, zoonotic disease control, and animal welfare advocacy. Veterinarians contribute to a harmonious coexistence between humans and animals, bridging gaps in understanding and forging bonds based on care and compassion.

The responsibilities of a veterinarian are as varied as the species they care for. From household pets to livestock and wildlife, veterinarians provide a spectrum of services that encompass preventive care, diagnostics, treatment, surgery, and emergency response. They administer vaccinations, conduct health check-ups, perform surgeries, and provide counseling to pet owners. Veterinarians also play a pivotal role in public health by monitoring and preventing the transmission of diseases from animals to humans, as well as ensuring the safety of the food supply through inspections and oversight of livestock health.

Being a veterinarian demands a unique blend of medical expertise, diagnostic skills, and interpersonal finesse. They must exhibit a deep understanding of animal anatomy, physiology, and pharmacology to diagnose and treat a wide array of conditions. Effective communication skills are crucial, enabling veterinarians to explain complex medical concepts to pet owners and ensure compliance with treatment plans. Empathy and compassion form the bedrock of their interactions, as veterinarians often work with pet owners during emotionally challenging times.

The life of a veterinarian is not without its challenges. The demands of the profession can lead to long hours, with emergency cases requiring attention at any time. Dealing with animals in distress or facing terminal illnesses can be emotionally taxing. Additionally, the financial burden of education and establishing a practice can be significant. However, the rewards are profound. The satisfaction of seeing a sick animal recover, the bond formed with grateful pet owners, and the knowledge that one has positively impacted both animal and human lives are among the many gratifying aspects of the profession.

In conclusion, being a veterinarian is a noble journey that transcends the boundaries of medicine and compassion. Veterinarians stand as pillars of health and well-being for animals, serving as guardians of both individual pets and broader animal populations. Their role extends beyond medical expertise; they advocate for animal rights, educate the public on responsible pet ownership, and contribute to the harmony of ecosystems. Despite the challenges, the rewards of witnessing animals thrive under their care, the opportunity to forge connections with pet owners, and the knowledge that they are a voice for those who cannot speak create a deeply fulfilling career. Veterinarians are the unsung heroes of the animal kingdom, embodying a commitment to healing, empathy, and the preservation of life in all its forms.

Into the Wild: The Life of a Zoologist

Zoologists, the modern-day adventurers of the natural world, delve into the mysteries of animal life, behavior, and ecosystems. With their profound curiosity, scientific rigor, and unwavering passion, they navigate diverse landscapes to understand the intricate tapestry of life on Earth. This section adventures into the realm of a zoologist, exploring the significance of their role, the multifaceted responsibilities they shoulder, the skills they hone, the challenges they tackle, and the sense of awe that accompanies those who study and protect the animal kingdom.

Zoologists are the guardians of our connection to the natural world, unraveling the secrets of animal behaviors, habitats, and interactions. Their work contributes to biodiversity conservation, ecosystem management, and our understanding of evolution. By studying the lives of animals, zoologists enrich our knowledge of the environment, facilitating informed decisions that safeguard both wildlife and human interests. Moreover, their research has the potential to inspire conservation efforts, educate the public, and foster a sense of empathy toward the creatures with which we share our planet.

The responsibilities of a zoologist encompass a wide spectrum, from field research to conservation advocacy. Zoologists conduct fieldwork, studying animals in their natural habitats to document behaviors, gather data, and observe interactions with the environment. They analyze collected samples and data, contributing to scientific knowledge about species' biology, genetics, and adaptations. Zoologists also design and implement conservation strategies, advocating for the protection of threatened species and the preservation of ecosystems.

Being a successful zoologist demands a blend of scientific

skills, adaptability, and a profound connection to nature. Zoologists must possess a deep understanding of biology, ecology, and genetics to interpret animal behaviors, migrations, and populations. Proficiency in data collection methods, including GPS tracking, camera traps, and molecular analyses, enhances their ability to draw accurate conclusions from fieldwork. Effective communication skills are crucial for sharing findings with fellow scientists, policymakers, and the public, driving awareness and action toward conservation goals.

The life of a zoologist is not without its challenges. Fieldwork often involves physically demanding conditions, ranging from extreme climates to remote and difficult-to-access locations. Long hours of observation, data collection, and analysis require patience and dedication. Additionally, funding for research and conservation efforts can be competitive and unpredictable. However, the rewards are profound. The thrill of discovering new species, contributing to scientific knowledge, and witnessing conservation successes creates a sense of purpose that transcends challenges. The opportunity to witness elusive animal behaviors, contribute to global conservation efforts, and inspire the next generation of nature enthusiasts adds layers of fulfillment to the profession.

In conclusion, being a zoologist is a journey of exploration, understanding, and preservation. Zoologists act as stewards of the natural world, unraveling the intricate stories of animals and ecosystems. Their significance extends beyond science; they are the ambassadors of the animal kingdom, advocating for its protection and illuminating its wonders. Despite the challenges, the rewards of unveiling hidden secrets, driving conservation efforts, and nurturing a deeper connection between humanity and nature make being a zoologist a profoundly meaningful career choice. Zoologists stand as custodians of biodiversity, embodying the wonder, respect, and responsibility that come with the study and protection of life on our planet.

Illuminating Pathways: Navigating the Circuitry of Being an Electrician

Being an electrician is an indispensable and multifaceted occupation that powers modern society. Electricians are the unsung heroes behind the scenes, ensuring that the world remains illuminated, connected, and functioning smoothly. This section delves into the captivating realm of being an electrician, unveiling the motivations that lead individuals to pursue this trade, the technical expertise required, the challenges faced in a rapidly evolving field, and the immense satisfaction derived from providing essential services that impact daily lives.

Becoming an electrician is often ignited by a fascination with electricity's boundless applications and a drive to understand the intricacies of electrical systems. The allure of manipulating currents, generating power, and unraveling the mysteries of circuits and components captivates individuals early on. Electricians play a vital role in virtually every aspect of modern life, from lighting up homes to powering industries, and their expertise is indispensable in maintaining the complex web of electrical infrastructure. The electrical field attracts those with a strong aptitude for problem-solving, a keen eye for detail, and a desire to contribute to the technological progress that shapes the world.

The journey of an electrician is a journey of technical mastery, where theoretical knowledge intertwines with hands-on skills. Electricians undergo comprehensive training to understand the principles of electrical theory, safety regulations, and the intricacies of electrical systems. They learn to interpret blueprints, install wiring, and troubleshoot complex electrical issues. The artistry lies in their ability to transform abstract concepts into tangible solutions, whether it's wiring a residential building or maintaining industrial machinery. The electrician's toolkit encompasses a diverse array of skills, from handling electrical tools and equipment to staying updated with the latest advancements in technology.

The field of electrical work is in a constant state of evolution, with technological advancements shaping the way electricians approach their craft. As smart systems, renewable energy sources, and energy-efficient technologies become the norm, electricians must adapt to new paradigms. They are at the forefront of integrating these innovations into existing systems, ensuring seamless functionality while maximizing energy efficiency. The challenge lies in staying up-to-date with evolving codes, standards, and safety protocols to deliver high-quality and reliable services. Electricians must balance traditional expertise with a willingness to embrace change, positioning themselves as essential contributors to a sustainable and technologically advanced future.

The electrician's journey is not without its challenges, chief among them being safety. Working with electrical currents and equipment requires meticulous attention to safety protocols to prevent accidents and hazards. Electricians often work in diverse environments, from residential settings to industrial sites, each presenting unique risks. They must stay vigilant in identifying potential hazards, using protective gear, and adhering to established guidelines. Additionally, troubleshooting electrical issues demands analytical thinking, as electricians must trace the source of problems and devise effective solutions swiftly. The technical complexity and responsibility of the work can be mentally and physically demanding, underscoring the need for continuous training and awareness.

The fulfillment derived from being an electrician goes beyond technical expertise; it encompasses the impact made on individuals and communities. Electricians enable people to live and work comfortably, ensuring that homes are well-lit, appliances function, and industries operate smoothly. Their work is essential in emergencies, such as power outages or electrical faults, where rapid response can prevent disruptions. Electricians serve as problem-solvers, assisting clients in making informed decisions about electrical installations, repairs, and upgrades. The satisfaction of successfully diagnosing and resolving electrical issues, along with the gratitude of those who benefit from their services, adds a profound sense of purpose to the electrician's role.

In conclusion, being an electrician is a dynamic journey that blends technical mastery, adaptability, and a commitment to safety. Electricians are the architects of the invisible infrastructure that powers our modern world. The technical craftsmanship they bring to their work is the foundation of their success, allowing them to navigate the complexities of electrical systems with precision. As the field continues to evolve, electricians find themselves at the forefront of innovation, embracing new technologies while upholding stringent safety standards. Ultimately, the significance of their role lies not only in their technical expertise but also in the tangible impact they have on people's lives, ensuring that the lights stay on, machinery runs smoothly, and society remains interconnected. Being an electrician is a testament to the power of knowledge, skill, and service that keeps the world charged and illuminated.

Engineering Horizons: Navigating Innovation and Problem-Solving

Being an engineer is a transformative journey that shapes the world through innovation, problem-solving, and a commitment to progress. Engineers are the architects of modern society, responsible for designing and implementing solutions that improve our lives in countless ways. This section dives into the captivating realm of being an engineer, exploring the motivations that drive individuals to choose this path, the diverse fields within engineering, the challenges engineers face, and the profound satisfaction of contributing to technological advancement and societal betterment.

Becoming an engineer often springs from an innate curiosity about how things work and a desire to make a tangible impact on the world. Engineers are driven by a fascination with problem-solving, an eagerness to tackle complex challenges, and a thirst for innovation. The seeds of engineering passion are often sown in childhood, as individuals tinker with gadgets, take apart appliances, or dream up inventions. The allure of engineering lies in its multidisciplinary nature, encompassing fields as diverse as mechanical, civil, electrical, and software engineering. This profession attracts those with an analytical mindset, a flair for creativity, and a relentless pursuit of excellence.

The realm of engineering is vast and encompasses a wide range of specialties, each with its unique focus and application. Mechanical engineers design and build everything from intricate machinery to cutting-edge vehicles. Civil engineers shape the physical infrastructure of societies, crafting roads, bridges, and buildings that stand as testaments to human achievement. Electrical engineers harness the power of electricity, driving technological advancements and enabling innovations in communication, energy, and electronics. Software engineers develop the digital landscapes we inhabit, creating applications and systems that power our interconnected world. Each engineering field presents its own challenges and rewards, catering to diverse interests and skill sets.

The journey of an engineer is not without its challenges. Engineers are tasked with navigating complexity, translating theoretical concepts into practical solutions, and ensuring that their designs are safe, efficient, and sustainable. The iterative nature of engineering demands continuous improvement, where prototypes are refined and optimized to meet rigorous standards. Additionally, engineers often collaborate across disciplines, necessitating effective communication and an ability to work in teams. The pressure to innovate and deliver solutions on time can be mentally and emotionally demanding, underscoring the importance of resilience and adaptability in the engineering profession.

The essence of being an engineer lies in the satisfaction of seeing ideas evolve into tangible solutions that shape the future. The ability to design products, systems, and structures that enhance efficiency, convenience, and quality of life is profoundly rewarding. Engineers contribute to technological breakthroughs that transform industries, from medical devices that save lives to sustainable energy solutions that address environmental challenges. Witnessing their creations in action, knowing they've played a role in societal progress, fuels a deep sense of purpose. The fulfillment derived from turning concepts into reality fuels engineers' drive to continuously push boundaries and elevate human potential.

Beyond technical expertise, being an engineer carries an ethical responsibility. Engineers hold the power to influence society and impact lives on a grand scale. This responsibility demands a commitment to ethical practices, ensuring that the innovations they create align with the greater good. Engineers must consider the social and environmental implications of their designs, striving to minimize negative impacts while maximizing benefits. The ethos of responsible engineering underscores the profession's role in safeguarding human welfare, promoting sustainability, and contributing to equitable progress.

In conclusion, being an engineer is a transformative journey that fuses innovation, problem-solving, and a commitment to societal advancement. Engineers are architects of progress, shaping the future through their technical expertise and creative prowess. The diverse specialties within engineering cater to a wide array of interests and talents, fostering a dynamic and intellectually stimulating profession. Challenges are met with tenacity, adaptability, and the drive to overcome complexity. The profound satisfaction of contributing to technological advancements and the betterment of society underscores the significance of engineering as a vocation that fuels progress and elevates the human experience. As engineers forge ahead, they stand as beacons of innovation, carrying the torch of human ingenuity into uncharted territories of possibility.

Flowing Expertise: Navigating the World of Plumbing and Piping

Being a plumber is a vital and intricate profession that ensures the smooth functioning of our daily lives. Plumbers are the unsung heroes who maintain the intricate network of pipes, valves, and fixtures that provide us with clean water and efficient drainage. This section explores into the captivating realm of being a plumber, exploring the motivations that lead individuals to choose this trade, the technical expertise required, the challenges faced in diverse plumbing scenarios, and the immense satisfaction derived from solving complex problems that impact public health and comfort.

Becoming a plumber often springs from a blend of practicality, curiosity, and a desire to make a tangible impact on communities. Plumbers are essential figures in maintaining public health, safety, and hygiene by ensuring proper water supply and waste disposal. The profession often attracts those who enjoy working with their hands, possess a knack for problem-solving, and appreciate the intrinsic satisfaction that comes from fixing issues that directly impact people's lives. The significance of plumbing transcends its technical aspects, encompassing the crucial role plumbers play in ensuring the well-being and comfort of society.

The journey of a plumber is one of technical mastery, encompassing an array of skills that range from basic pipe fitting to complex system design. Plumbers undergo comprehensive training to grasp the fundamentals of plumbing systems, water distribution, drainage, and safety codes. They learn to read blueprints, install and repair piping, and troubleshoot a myriad of issues that arise in residential, commercial, and industrial settings. The artistry lies in their ability to quickly diagnose problems, devise efficient solutions, and execute repairs with precision. Plumbers wield a versatile toolkit that includes traditional tools, modern equipment, and an ever-expanding knowledge of the latest technologies.

Being a plumber presents an array of challenges due to the diverse nature of plumbing scenarios. Plumbers must be prepared to encounter a wide range of issues, from minor leaks and clogged drains to intricate problems involving water heaters, sewage systems, and complex pipe networks. They often work in conditions that require flexibility and adaptability, as no two plumbing jobs are the same. Plumbers must also navigate time-sensitive situations, such as burst pipes or malfunctioning water heaters, where swift action is essential to prevent further damage. The ability to troubleshoot on the spot, devise effective solutions, and remain composed under pressure is crucial to success in the plumbing profession.

The satisfaction derived from being a plumber is deeply rooted in the act of problem-solving. Plumbers are akin to detectives, uncovering the source of leaks, blockages, and malfunctions and devising strategies to rectify them. The moment when water begins to flow smoothly through once-clogged pipes or when a persistent leak is finally resolved is immensely gratifying. Plumbers often witness the immediate impact of their work, as their efforts restore comfort and functionality to homes, businesses, and public spaces. The ability to address pressing issues and contribute to the well-being of individuals and communities imparts a strong sense of purpose to the plumbing profession.

Beyond the technical aspects, being a plumber carries an ethical dimension. Plumbers are instrumental in safeguarding public health by ensuring clean water supply and proper waste disposal. Their work plays a crucial role in preventing the spread of waterborne diseases and maintaining sanitary living conditions. Additionally, plumbers contribute to environmental conservation by promoting water efficiency and reducing wastage. The commitment to these responsibilities underscores the vital role plumbers play in upholding community well-being, highlighting the ethical imperative that guides their actions.

In conclusion, being a plumber is a dynamic and indispensable journey that involves technical expertise, problem-solving acumen, and a commitment to public health and comfort. Plumbers are the architects of functional plumbing systems that sustain our daily lives. The profession is a blend of artistry and science, requiring a versatile skill set and the ability to adapt to diverse challenges. Plumbers find fulfillment in their role as problem-solvers, witnessing the immediate impact of their work as they restore order and functionality to plumbing systems. Beyond the technical intricacies, the ethical dimension of plumbing underscores its significance in maintaining public health and promoting environmental sustainability. As plumbers navigate the intricacies of pipes, valves, and fixtures, they carry the torch of reliability, comfort, and safety that underpins modern society.

Fusing Creativity and Precision: Exploring the Craft of Being a Welder

Being a welder is a transformative journey that fuses technical expertise, creativity, and craftsmanship. Welders are the skilled artisans who join metal components, creating strong and durable connections that form the backbone of various industries. This section adventures into the captivating world of being a welder, uncovering the motivations that lead individuals to choose this profession, the intricate process of welding, the challenges faced in mastering this craft, and the profound satisfaction derived from turning raw materials into structures that shape our world.

Becoming a welder often emerges from a blend of practicality, curiosity, and a desire to transform raw materials into functional and aesthetic creations. Welding is an ancient practice that has evolved with technology, making it a cornerstone of modern manufacturing and construction. The allure of welding lies in its transformative power – the ability to turn individual metal pieces into cohesive structures that withstand the test of time. Welders often possess a natural affinity for working with their hands, a keen eye for detail, and a fascination with the marriage of science and artistry that welding entails. The significance of welding goes beyond the technical aspects, encompassing the integral role welders play in constructing everything from skyscrapers to intricate sculptures.

The journey of a welder is a delicate dance between precision and creativity. Welders must master a range of techniques, from arc welding to gas welding, each demanding meticulous attention to detail. The welding process involves melting metals at high temperatures and fusing them together to create seamless connections. This demands not only technical expertise in understanding various metals, their properties, and the appropriate welding methods but also the ability to envision the end result. Creative intuition guides welders as they determine the ideal welding position, filler materials, and the aesthetic quality of the finished weld. The artistry lies in finding the perfect balance between structural integrity and visual appeal.

The path of a welder is not without its challenges, chief among them being the demand for meticulous precision. Even the smallest flaw in a weld can compromise the structural integrity of a project. Welders must work in varied environments – from construction sites to manufacturing facilities – often contending with challenging weather conditions, tight spaces, and physically demanding tasks. Additionally, different metals require different welding techniques, demanding a deep understanding of metallurgy and the properties of each material. Welding also carries safety concerns due to the intense heat and the potential for exposure to fumes. The pursuit of perfection in welding requires constant learning, adaptability, and a commitment to honing one's skills.

The essence of being a welder lies in the satisfaction of seeing individual pieces of metal come together to form a cohesive whole. Welders are the silent contributors to our built environment, playing a pivotal role in the construction of infrastructure, vehicles, and machinery that drive progress. The fulfillment derived from creating structures that endure the test of time and contribute to society's development is deeply rewarding. Welders witness their work in the girders of bridges, the pipelines of industries, and the intricate designs of sculptures. The tangible impact of their craftsmanship fuels a sense of accomplishment that transcends words.

Beyond the physical manifestations, being a welder holds a unique significance in shaping the world we inhabit. Welders enable industries to thrive by fabricating machinery and equipment that power production. They contribute to the creation of structures that define urban landscapes and ensure the functionality of vehicles that connect us. Furthermore, the artistic dimension of welding is showcased in sculptures, artwork, and decorative structures that beautify public spaces. Welders play a pivotal role in modernizing infrastructure, enhancing safety, and driving innovation. Their work is a testament to the union of art and science, shaping the world through connections that withstand the test of time.

In conclusion, being a welder is a transformative journey that merges precision, creativity, and craftsmanship. Welders are the architects of connections, forging metal components that form the backbone of industries and structures. The journey of a welder is marked by technical expertise, adaptability, and a relentless pursuit of perfection. Challenges are met with resilience, as welders navigate various welding techniques, materials, and environmental conditions. The profound satisfaction of witnessing their work in action fuels a sense of accomplishment that transcends words. Beyond the physical impact, the work of welders shapes the world, underpinning progress, innovation, and the visual beauty of the environments we inhabit. As welders fuse metal components, they also fuse the elements of artistry, science, and craftsmanship into a craft that stands as a cornerstone of modern society.

Precision Mechanics: Navigating the Intricate World of Automotive Expertise

Being a mechanic is a dynamic and indispensable profession that keeps the world moving by ensuring the reliability and functionality of vehicles. Mechanics are the skilled artisans who diagnose, repair, and maintain a diverse range of vehicles, from cars and trucks to motorcycles and heavy machinery. This section delves into the captivating realm of being a mechanic, exploring the motivations that lead individuals to choose this trade, the technical expertise required, the challenges encountered in diagnosing and repairing complex systems, and the profound satisfaction derived from restoring vehicles to optimal performance.

Becoming a mechanic often emerges from a combination of hands-on curiosity, problem-solving aptitude, and a deep-rooted fascination with machines. Mechanics are the unsung heroes of transportation, responsible for keeping vehicles operational and safe. The allure of the profession lies in the blend of technical expertise, analytical thinking, and the ability to troubleshoot intricate mechanical and electrical systems. Mechanics are driven by a desire to understand the inner workings of vehicles, to solve puzzles that arise from mechanical issues, and to contribute to the well-being and safety of vehicle owners. The significance of mechanics transcends their technical roles, as they play a vital part in maintaining societal mobility.

The journey of a mechanic is a journey of technical mastery, encompassing a wide range of skills that span from engine diagnostics to electrical repairs. Mechanics undergo comprehensive training to gain a deep understanding of vehicle systems, including engines, transmissions, braking systems, and electronic components. They learn to interpret diagnostic codes, use specialized tools, and apply their expertise to solve complex problems. The artistry lies in their ability to decipher symptoms, identify root causes, and execute repairs with precision. Mechanics wield a versatile toolkit that includes traditional mechanical tools and sophisticated diagnostic equipment, adapting to the rapid technological advancements in the automotive industry.

Being a mechanic presents a myriad of challenges due to the intricate nature of modern vehicles. Vehicles are equipped with sophisticated electronic systems, advanced safety features, and intricate engine components that demand specialized expertise. Mechanics must decipher diagnostic codes, address issues with precision, and adapt to evolving vehicle technologies. Moreover, they often work in fast-paced environments where time is of the essence, especially in emergency repair situations. The challenge lies in staying updated with the latest advancements, adapting to the unique characteristics of different vehicle makes and models, and providing efficient solutions that restore vehicles to optimal performance.

The essence of being a mechanic is the satisfaction derived from restoring vehicles to their full potential. Mechanics witness the tangible impact of their work as they transform malfunctioning machines into roadworthy vehicles. The moment an engine roars back to life, brakes function smoothly, or a persistent electrical issue is resolved, mechanics experience a sense of accomplishment that is both gratifying and fulfilling. The ability to solve problems that others may find daunting, to diagnose issues accurately, and to bring vehicles back to life is a testament to the expertise and dedication that mechanics bring to their craft.

Beyond the technical dimensions, being a mechanic carries a deeper significance in fostering trust and enabling societal mobility. Mechanics are the pillars of the transportation industry, ensuring that vehicles operate reliably and safely. Vehicle owners entrust mechanics with their most valuable possessions, relying on their expertise to keep their vehicles operational. This trust is built on the mechanic's commitment to honesty, transparency, and professionalism. Mechanics play a pivotal role in promoting road safety and contributing to the overall functionality of society. Their work is not just about fixing machines; it's about enabling individuals to navigate their lives with confidence and ease.

In conclusion, being a mechanic is a transformative journey that intertwines technical mastery, problem-solving skills, and a commitment to vehicular functionality. Mechanics are the heartbeats of transportation, breathing life into vehicles and enabling individuals to move seamlessly through their daily lives. The journey of a mechanic is marked by a passion for machines, a pursuit of technical expertise, and an unwavering dedication to solving intricate mechanical and electrical puzzles. Challenges are met with resilience and adaptability, as mechanics navigate the complexities of modern vehicles and embrace rapid technological advancements. The fulfillment derived from restoring vehicles to optimal performance underscores the significance of their role in society. Mechanics stand as the gatekeepers of mobility, the guardians of road safety, and the enablers of trust that propel the world forward on wheels of expertise and commitment.

Reviving Beauty: The Craftsmanship of an Auto Body Collision Repair Technician

Auto Body Collision Repair Technicians are the artisans who breathe new life into damaged vehicles, restoring them to their former glory after accidents. With their skilled hands and precision tools, they wield a unique blend of craftsmanship and technical expertise to mend dented frames, repair damaged panels, and transform wreckage into works of art. This section dives into the world of an Auto Body Collision Repair Technician, exploring the significance of their role, the intricate responsibilities they bear, the specialized skills they master, the challenges they face, and the satisfaction derived from resurrecting automobiles to their pristine condition.

Auto Body Collision Repair Technicians hold a crucial role in the automotive industry by salvaging vehicles that have met with accidents. They extend the lifespan of automobiles, sparing them from being written off as total losses. In doing so, they contribute to reducing waste and conserving resources. Beyond the environmental impact, these technicians play a vital part in restoring the safety and aesthetics of vehicles, ensuring they meet safety standards and regain their original beauty.

The responsibilities of an Auto Body Collision Repair Technician encompass a diverse array of tasks. They begin by assessing the extent of damage, identifying the repairs required, and developing a plan for restoration. Technicians skillfully dismantle damaged components, weld or reshape frames, replace or repair panels, and address issues with alignment and suspension. The meticulous attention to detail extends to painting and finishing, where technicians blend colors seamlessly and restore the vehicle's luster. Additionally, they collaborate with insurance adjusters and communicate with vehicle owners to provide a comprehensive service.

Being an Auto Body Collision Repair Technician demands a blend of technical proficiency and artistic finesse. Mastery of specialized tools, such as welding equipment and pneumatic tools, is essential for precision work. Technicians must understand automotive anatomy, structural integrity, and materials science to make informed repair decisions. Beyond the technical aspects, creative skills come into play when blending paint and restoring the vehicle's aesthetic appeal. Effective communication skills facilitate interactions with clients and colleagues, ensuring clarity in explaining repair processes and addressing concerns.

The life of an Auto Body Collision Repair Technician is not without its challenges. Repairing extensively damaged vehicles requires problem-solving skills and ingenuity to restore structural integrity. Working with diverse vehicle models demands adaptability to varying designs and technologies. The physically demanding nature of the job, including lifting heavy parts and working in uncomfortable positions, can take a toll on the body. However, the rewards are profound. The satisfaction of seeing a once-damaged vehicle transformed into a pristine condition, the gratitude of vehicle owners who regain their treasured possessions, and the pride in mastering a skill that blends craftsmanship and technology create a sense of fulfillment unique to this profession.

In conclusion, being an Auto Body Collision Repair Technician is a journey of creativity, skill, and precision that breathes new life into damaged vehicles. These technicians serve as both artists and mechanics, melding technical proficiency with artistic vision to restore vehicles to their former splendor. Their significance extends beyond the physical repairs; they play a pivotal role in extending the life of automobiles, reducing waste, and ensuring the safety of vehicles on the road. Despite the challenges, the rewards of witnessing the transformation of wreckage into a masterpiece, the sense of accomplishment in delivering high-quality repairs, and the knowledge that their work contributes to both aesthetics and safety make being an Auto Body Collision Repair Technician a fulfilling and vital career choice. These technicians stand as the guardians of renewal, shaping the vehicles that hold memories and aspirations for their owners.

Smiles and Wellness: Navigating Dentistry's Depths and Delights

Dentists, the guardians of oral health, play a vital role in ensuring the well-being of their patients' smiles. With a blend of medical expertise, technical skill, and empathy, they address dental issues, promote preventive care, and contribute to overall health. This section explores into the world of a dentist, exploring the significance of their role, the diverse responsibilities they shoulder, the skills they cultivate, the challenges they face, and the profound satisfaction they derive from restoring and maintaining healthy smiles.

Dentists hold a crucial position in healthcare, focusing on the intricate structure and function of the mouth and its impact on overall well-being. Beyond promoting a confident smile, oral health has direct connections to systemic health, including cardiovascular health and diabetes management. Dentists are instrumental in diagnosing and treating oral diseases, preventing dental issues, and enhancing the quality of life for their patients.

The responsibilities of a dentist encompass a wide range of tasks, spanning from routine check-ups to complex treatments. Dentists provide comprehensive oral examinations, diagnose conditions such as cavities and gum disease, and develop treatment plans tailored to each patient's needs. They perform restorative procedures such as fillings and crowns, as well as more specialized treatments like orthodontics and oral surgery. Additionally, dentists educate patients on oral hygiene practices, dietary habits, and lifestyle choices that contribute to optimal dental health.

Being a dentist requires a blend of medical knowledge, technical skills, and interpersonal prowess. Dentists must have a deep understanding of dental anatomy, physiology, and pathology to diagnose and treat various oral conditions.

Proficiency in using specialized dental equipment, from X-ray machines to precision instruments, is essential for accurate diagnoses and effective treatments. Communication skills are vital for explaining procedures, addressing patient concerns, and establishing trust.

The life of a dentist is not without its challenges. Dental procedures can be physically demanding, requiring precision and attention to detail. Patients' anxieties and fears related to dental treatments can present emotional challenges, demanding empathy and the ability to put patients at ease. Moreover, the evolving landscape of dental technology and techniques demands continuous learning and adaptation. However, the rewards are substantial. The satisfaction of relieving patients' pain, restoring their smiles, and improving their quality of life is immeasurable. Building lasting relationships with patients and witnessing their transformation from dental issues to confident smiles create a sense of fulfillment unique to the profession.

In conclusion, being a dentist is a dynamic journey that combines medical expertise with compassionate care. Dentists serve as partners in maintaining oral health, preventing diseases, and enhancing overall well-being. Their significance extends beyond the realm of dentistry, as oral health is intricately linked to systemic health. Despite the challenges, the rewards of transforming patients' lives through pain relief, restoring functionality, and boosting confidence make being a dentist a deeply fulfilling and impactful career choice. Dentists stand as advocates for healthy smiles, embodying the pursuit of health, well-being, and self-assurance that comes with optimal oral care.

Compassion in Care: Navigating
the Path of a Nursing Journey

Being a nurse is a profound and transformative calling that combines compassion, expertise, and a commitment to healing. Nurses are the heartbeat of healthcare, providing critical support, care, and empathy to patients during some of their most vulnerable moments. This section adventures into the inspiring world of being a nurse, uncovering the motivations that lead individuals to pursue this noble profession, the multifaceted roles nurses play, the challenges they navigate in a demanding healthcare environment, and the immense satisfaction derived from making a positive impact on patients' lives.

Becoming a nurse often arises from a deep-seated desire to care for others, to make a tangible difference in the lives of patients, and to contribute to the field of healthcare. Nurses are the frontlines of medical care, acting as advocates, educators, and caregivers for patients of all ages and backgrounds. The allure of nursing lies in the privilege of being there for patients during moments of vulnerability, providing not only medical support but also emotional solace. The profession attracts individuals with a genuine passion for helping others, a strong sense of empathy, and the willingness to work in high-pressure environments. The significance of nursing transcends its technical aspects, encompassing the profound impact nurses have on patient outcomes and overall well-being.

The journey of a nurse is a dynamic one that involves a wide array of roles and responsibilities. Nurses act as caregivers, administering medications, monitoring patients' vital signs, and providing hands-on medical attention. They also serve as educators, explaining treatment plans, offering guidance on self-care, and equipping patients with the knowledge to manage their conditions. Nurses advocate for patients' rights, ensuring they receive the best care possible and that their voices are heard. Additionally, nurses collaborate with interdisciplinary teams, working alongside physicians, therapists, and social workers to provide comprehensive patient care. The versatility of nursing requires not only medical expertise but also strong communication, critical thinking, and organizational skills.

Being a nurse comes with its fair share of challenges, largely due to the fast-paced and ever-evolving nature of healthcare environments. Nurses work long shifts, often dealing with physically and emotionally demanding situations. The constant demand for attention, the need to make quick decisions, and the exposure to challenging medical cases can be mentally taxing. Moreover, nurses are confronted with ethical dilemmas, patient advocacy issues, and the challenge of maintaining a work-life balance. The ability to remain resilient, maintain composure under pressure, and find ways to cope with stress is essential in the nursing profession.

The essence of being a nurse lies in the fulfillment derived from making a positive impact on patients' lives. Nurses witness the transformation of patients from illness to recovery, from vulnerability to strength, and from fear to hope. The ability to alleviate pain, offer comfort, and provide emotional support can have a profound effect on patients' well-being. Nurses often build deep connections with patients and their families, offering a human touch that goes beyond the medical aspect of care. The satisfaction of knowing that their efforts contribute to improved patient outcomes and enhanced quality of life fuels nurses' sense of purpose and dedication.

Beyond the technical aspects, being a nurse embodies the heart of healthcare. Nurses play an integral role in shaping patient experiences, influencing the overall perception of medical care. They provide a bridge between medical professionals and patients, ensuring effective communication, trust, and empathy. The compassionate care nurses offer extends beyond physical health, encompassing emotional support, psychological comfort, and a listening ear. Nurses also advocate for public health initiatives, health education, and preventative measures, contributing to healthier communities. Their role as advocates, educators, caregivers, and healers underscores their significance as pillars of the healthcare system.

In conclusion, being a nurse is a transformative journey that marries compassion, expertise, and dedication. Nurses are the unsung heroes of healthcare, providing critical support, care, and empathy to patients during their most vulnerable moments. The journey of a nurse is marked by a genuine passion for helping others, a commitment to healing, and the ability to navigate multifaceted roles. Challenges are met with resilience and the unwavering commitment to patient well-being. The profound satisfaction of making a positive impact on patients' lives, offering comfort and hope in times of distress, and contributing to improved health outcomes underscores the profound significance of the nursing profession. As nurses navigate the complexities of healthcare, they stand as beacons of compassion and expertise, embodying the heart and soul of healing that shapes the lives of patients and communities.

Prescription for Excellence:
Navigating the Pharmacy Profession

Being a pharmacist is a profound and vital profession that bridges the gap between medical expertise and patient well-being. Pharmacists are the healthcare professionals who ensure the safe and effective use of medications, providing guidance, education, and personalized care to patients. This section delves into the intricate world of being a pharmacist, exploring the motivations that lead individuals to pursue this noble profession, the multifaceted responsibilities pharmacists undertake, the challenges they face in a rapidly evolving healthcare landscape, and the gratification derived from improving patients' health and quality of life.

Becoming a pharmacist is often born from a genuine desire to make a positive impact on patients' lives, to ensure the proper use of medications, and to contribute to the field of healthcare. Pharmacists are the guardians of medication safety, responsible for dispensing medications, reviewing prescriptions for accuracy, and offering guidance on potential drug interactions and side effects. The allure of the profession lies in the ability to provide personalized care, educate patients about their medications, and collaborate with other healthcare providers to optimize patient outcomes. The significance of pharmacists extends beyond their technical roles, as they play a critical part in promoting medication adherence, preventing adverse events, and enhancing overall patient well-being.

The journey of a pharmacist encompasses a diverse range of roles that extend beyond medication dispensing. Pharmacists are medication experts who review prescriptions, ensure appropriate dosages, and offer alternatives when necessary. They also serve as educators, providing patients with comprehensive information about their medications, including proper administration and potential side effects. Pharmacists collaborate with physicians and other healthcare professionals to optimize drug therapy, addressing individual patient needs and potential contraindications. Additionally, pharmacists play a pivotal role in promoting public health through initiatives such as immunizations and health screenings. The multifaceted nature of the pharmacist's role demands not only clinical expertise but also effective communication and interpersonal skills.

Being a pharmacist comes with a set of challenges, largely due to the evolving nature of healthcare and the complexities of the pharmaceutical industry. Pharmacists must stay updated with constantly changing drug information, new medications, and emerging research. They often encounter ethical dilemmas related to patient privacy, medication shortages, and insurance constraints. The role also involves addressing misconceptions about medications and combating misinformation that patients may encounter. The challenge lies in managing time effectively, staying current with medical advancements, and navigating the fine balance between patient care, administrative duties, and regulatory requirements.

The essence of being a pharmacist is the gratification derived from positively impacting patients' lives. Pharmacists witness the transformation of patients from uncertainty to understanding, from confusion to empowerment. The ability to alleviate patients' concerns, answer their questions, and ensure they are informed and confident about their medications is deeply rewarding. Pharmacists often build strong relationships with patients, serving as a consistent source of support and education. The satisfaction of knowing that their expertise contributes to improved health outcomes, reduced hospitalizations, and enhanced quality of life fuels a sense of purpose that extends beyond the professional realm.

Beyond the technical aspects, being a pharmacist embodies a pivotal role in healthcare systems. Pharmacists contribute to patient safety by preventing medication errors, offering counseling, and conducting medication reviews. They are essential in optimizing medication regimens, minimizing drug interactions, and ensuring that patients receive the most suitable treatments. Pharmacists also contribute to public health by promoting responsible medication use, advocating for health education, and participating in efforts to combat the misuse of medications. Their role as medication experts underscores their significance in promoting patient well-being, improving health literacy, and enhancing the overall effectiveness of healthcare systems.

In conclusion, being a pharmacist is a transformative journey that merges clinical expertise, patient care, and a commitment to health promotion. Pharmacists are the custodians of medication safety, playing a crucial role in ensuring patients receive appropriate treatments and understand their medications. The journey of a pharmacist is marked by a genuine passion for patient well-being, a commitment to accurate medication management, and the ability to navigate multifaceted roles. Challenges are met with resilience, adaptability, and an unwavering dedication to providing the best possible care. The profound satisfaction of positively impacting patients' health, enhancing medication adherence, and contributing to improved health outcomes underscores the profound significance of the pharmacist's role. As pharmacists dispense care and compassion, they stand as pillars of expertise, advocates for patient safety, and partners in promoting health and well-being within communities.

Guardians of Knowledge: Exploring the World of Being a Librarian

Being a librarian is a transformative and enlightening vocation that revolves around nurturing the exchange of knowledge, fostering a love for literature, and providing essential resources to communities. Librarians are the custodians of information, curating and organizing vast collections of books, digital media, and reference materials. This section dives into the intriguing world of being a librarian, exploring the motivations that lead individuals to choose this enriching profession, the multifaceted roles librarians undertake, the challenges they navigate in the digital age, and the profound satisfaction derived from empowering individuals through access to education and culture.

Becoming a librarian often emanates from a deep-rooted passion for literature, a commitment to preserving cultural heritage, and a genuine desire to facilitate learning. Librarians are the gatekeepers of knowledge, connecting individuals with the wealth of information that libraries offer. The allure of the profession lies in the ability to foster intellectual growth, inspire curiosity, and support lifelong learning. Librarians often possess a genuine love for books, a fascination with diverse topics, and a strong belief in the transformative power of education. The significance of librarians transcends their technical roles, as they play a pivotal part in nurturing literacy, promoting intellectual freedom, and shaping the intellectual landscape of communities.

The journey of a librarian encompasses a rich array of responsibilities that go beyond shelving books. Librarians curate collections, ensuring that libraries house materials that cater to the diverse needs and interests of their patrons. They serve as guides, assisting individuals in locating information, conducting research, and utilizing library resources effectively.

Librarians also engage in community outreach, organizing events, workshops, and reading programs that promote a love for reading and learning. In the digital age, librarians have evolved to manage electronic resources, offer technical assistance, and provide guidance in navigating the vast realm of online information. The multifaceted nature of the librarian's role demands not only a passion for learning but also strong interpersonal and organizational skills.

Being a librarian presents a unique set of challenges, particularly in the era of digital information. The proliferation of online resources has transformed the way individuals access information, posing challenges in evaluating the reliability and authenticity of sources. Librarians must adapt to technological advancements, offering guidance on digital literacy and assisting patrons in navigating the complex landscape of online databases and e-books. Moreover, budget constraints and evolving library needs require librarians to balance traditional print resources with digital collections. The challenge lies in maintaining the essence of a physical library while harnessing the potential of technology to enhance access and engagement.

The essence of being a librarian lies in the fulfillment derived from empowering individuals through knowledge and education. Librarians witness the transformation of patrons as they discover new worlds through literature, expand their horizons through research, and enhance their skills through educational resources. The ability to guide individuals toward finding answers, sparking curiosity, and fostering critical thinking is profoundly rewarding. Librarians often build connections with patrons, providing a supportive environment where learning is nurtured and intellectual growth is encouraged. The satisfaction of knowing that their efforts contribute to the intellectual and personal development of individuals fuels a sense of purpose that extends beyond the professional realm.

Beyond the technical aspects, being a librarian carries a unique significance in preserving cultural heritage and building vibrant communities. Librarians are cultural stewards, preserving books, documents, and artifacts that offer insights into history and society. They organize events that celebrate literature, arts, and culture, fostering a sense of community and inclusivity. Librarians also promote access to information, ensuring that libraries serve as democratic spaces where individuals of all backgrounds can engage with diverse ideas and perspectives. Their role as facilitators of dialogue, champions of education, and guardians of free expression underscores their significance in shaping informed and enlightened societies.

In conclusion, being a librarian is a transformative journey that marries a passion for knowledge with a commitment to fostering lifelong learning. Librarians are the torchbearers of education, connecting individuals with a universe of information and culture. The journey of a librarian is marked by a deep appreciation for literature, a dedication to intellectual empowerment, and the ability to navigate multifaceted roles. Challenges are met with adaptability, creativity, and a relentless pursuit of enhancing access to resources. The profound satisfaction of witnessing patrons embark on intellectual journeys, discover new passions, and grow as individuals underscores the profound significance of the librarian's role. As librarians curate knowledge, kindle curiosity, and foster a love for learning, they stand as cultural custodians and community builders who illuminate the path to wisdom and enlightenment.

Unlocking Dream Homes: The Realities of a Real Estate Agent

Real estate agents, the architects of property transactions, play a pivotal role in connecting individuals with their ideal homes and investment opportunities. With their in-depth knowledge of the market, negotiation skills, and dedication to client satisfaction, they guide buyers and sellers through the complex landscape of real estate transactions. This section explores into the realm of a real estate agent, exploring the significance of their role, the diverse responsibilities they undertake, the skills they master, the challenges they navigate, and the sense of fulfillment they derive from turning properties into homes.

Real estate agents are more than intermediaries; they are the linchpins of real estate transactions. They bridge the gap between sellers looking to offload their properties and buyers seeking their dream homes. Agents provide valuable insights into market trends, property values, and investment opportunities. Their expertise ensures that buyers find properties that align with their preferences, while sellers receive fair market value for their assets. Ultimately, real estate agents facilitate the realization of people's aspirations, whether it's finding a first home, upgrading to a larger space, or making sound investments.

The responsibilities of a real estate agent are multifaceted and encompass the entire spectrum of property transactions. Agents conduct market research to accurately price properties and determine their marketability. They market properties through various channels, from online listings to open houses, to attract potential buyers. Agents guide clients through negotiations, presenting offers and counteroffers to secure favorable deals. They also handle the intricate legal and paperwork aspects of transactions, ensuring that all legal requirements are met and transactions proceed smoothly. The role of an agent extends beyond sales; they serve as advisors, offering insights on property maintenance, market trends, and investment strategies.

Being a real estate agent demands a diverse skill set that goes beyond property knowledge. Effective communication is paramount; agents must clearly convey information, answer client questions, and negotiate terms. Problem-solving skills come into play when overcoming challenges during transactions, such as financing issues or unexpected property defects. Agents must also exhibit strong interpersonal skills, as building trust and rapport with clients is essential. Additionally, technological proficiency is crucial in the digital age, where agents utilize online platforms and tools to market properties and streamline transactions.

The life of a real estate agent is not without its challenges. The industry can be highly competitive, with agents vying for clients and listings in a saturated market. The unpredictability of the market can lead to fluctuations in business, and the demanding nature of the job often involves irregular working hours, including evenings and weekends. Furthermore, the emotional investment in clients' aspirations and the complexities of negotiations can be mentally taxing. However, the rewards are substantial. The satisfaction of helping clients find their dream homes, the thrill of closing a successful deal, and the potential for substantial financial rewards make being a real estate agent a gratifying career choice.

In conclusion, a career as a real estate agent is a dynamic journey that blends market expertise, negotiation skills, and client-centric service. Agents play an essential role in transforming properties into homes, connecting buyers with spaces that resonate with their lifestyles and aspirations. They contribute to economic growth by facilitating property transactions that invigorate local markets. Despite the challenges, the rewards of fulfilling dreams, witnessing the joy of clients achieving their homeownership goals, and playing a central role in one of life's most significant decisions make being a real estate agent a fulfilling and impactful profession. Real estate agents are the conduits of change, turning properties into havens and shaping the fabric of communities through their dedication and expertise.

Crafting Dreams: Exploring the Artistry of Being a Carpenter

Being a carpenter is a transformative and artistic endeavor that involves working with wood to create functional and aesthetic structures. Carpenters are the skilled craftsmen who bring architectural designs to life, constructing everything from houses and furniture to intricate woodworking projects. This section adventures into the captivating world of being a carpenter, uncovering the motivations that lead individuals to pursue this age-old profession, the technical expertise required, the challenges encountered in mastering woodworking techniques, and the profound satisfaction derived from transforming raw materials into enduring pieces of art.

Becoming a carpenter often stems from a blend of creative curiosity, a fascination with woodworking, and a desire to shape the physical world with one's hands. Carpenters are the architects of wood, crafting structures that are both utilitarian and visually appealing. The allure of the profession lies in the ability to take raw materials and mold them into functional and beautiful creations. Carpenters often possess a keen eye for detail, a natural affinity for working with tools, and a deep appreciation for the intrinsic qualities of wood. The significance of carpentry transcends its technical aspects, encompassing the artistry of bringing designs to life and the enduring impact of structures that stand as a testament to craftsmanship.

The journey of a carpenter is a journey of technical mastery, involving a range of skills that span from measuring and cutting wood to intricate joinery and finishing techniques. Carpenters undergo comprehensive training to understand wood types, their properties, and the various tools and techniques used in woodworking. They learn to read blueprints, calculate measurements, and create precise cuts that fit seamlessly together. The artistry lies in their ability to envision the end product, select the appropriate wood species, and execute precise joinery that results in a sturdy and visually appealing structure. Carpenters work with a versatile set of tools, ranging from traditional hand tools to modern power tools that enhance efficiency and precision.

Being a carpenter presents an array of challenges due to the complexities of working with wood. Wood is a natural material that responds to changes in temperature, humidity, and moisture content, leading to potential warping, splitting, or shrinkage. Carpenters must adapt to these variables, selecting the right techniques and materials to ensure the longevity of their creations. Moreover, carpenters work with various wood species, each with distinct properties that require specific handling and finishing techniques. The challenge lies in achieving precision in measurements, executing complex joinery, and crafting pieces that are both functional and aesthetically pleasing. Carpenters must also prioritize safety, using tools correctly and adhering to safety protocols to prevent accidents.

The essence of being a carpenter lies in the satisfaction of creating beauty and functionality from raw materials. Carpenters witness the transformation of wood into intricate pieces of furniture, architectural elements, and structures that serve practical purposes. The moment when a piece of wood is meticulously shaped and assembled, resulting in a perfectly fitted joint or a gracefully designed furniture piece, is immensely gratifying. Carpenters often experience a strong sense of accomplishment as they see their creations enhance spaces and elevate the quality of life for individuals who interact with their work. The tangible impact of their craftsmanship fosters a deep sense of pride and fulfillment.

Beyond the technical intricacies, being a carpenter carries the responsibility of preserving tradition while embracing innovation. Carpenters often draw inspiration from historical designs and techniques, infusing them with modern sensibilities to create pieces that are both timeless and contemporary. The role of a carpenter extends beyond construction to cultural preservation, as they contribute to the continuity of woodworking traditions that have shaped human history. Moreover, carpenters adapt to technological advancements, incorporating modern tools and techniques that enhance efficiency and precision. The balance between tradition and innovation underscores the dynamic nature of carpentry, making it a craft that bridges the past and the future.

In conclusion, being a carpenter is a transformative journey that melds technical mastery, artistic expression, and a commitment to craftsmanship. Carpenters are the sculptors of wood, transforming raw materials into functional and visually captivating structures. The journey of a carpenter is marked by a deep appreciation for the beauty of wood, a dedication to precision, and the ability to navigate challenges inherent in working with a natural material. Challenges are met with adaptability, problem-solving skills, and a relentless pursuit of perfection. The profound satisfaction of seeing wood transformed into enduring pieces of art, witnessing the impact of their creations on spaces and individuals, underscores the profound significance of the carpenter's role. As carpenters shape wood, they also shape environments, infusing spaces with beauty, functionality, and the timeless essence of craftsmanship.

Precision Craftsmanship:
Exploring the Art and Science
of Being a Machinist

Being a machinist is a transformative and essential endeavor that involves the creation of intricate components and precision parts used in a wide range of industries. Machinists are skilled craftsmen who operate machinery to shape, cut, and fabricate materials into precise specifications. This section delves into the captivating world of being a machinist, uncovering the motivations that lead individuals to choose this profession, the technical expertise required, the challenges encountered in manipulating complex machinery, and the deep satisfaction derived from crafting objects that drive innovation and progress.

Becoming a machinist often emerges from a blend of curiosity, problem-solving aptitude, and a fascination with the intricacies of machinery. Machinists are the architects of precision, responsible for translating design blueprints into functional parts that power industries. The allure of the profession lies in the ability to transform raw materials into components that meet exact specifications, contributing to the advancement of technology and manufacturing. Machinists often possess an innate mechanical aptitude, an eye for detail, and a passion for creating objects that operate seamlessly. The significance of machinists extends beyond their technical roles, as they play a pivotal part in driving innovation, enhancing productivity, and shaping the modern world.

The journey of a machinist is marked by technical mastery, encompassing a range of skills that span from operating machine tools to interpreting complex engineering drawings. Machinists undergo rigorous training to understand the principles of machining, metallurgy, and the properties of various materials. They learn to operate specialized machinery such as lathes, mills, and CNC (Computer Numerical Control) equipment with precision. The artistry lies in their ability to calibrate machines, select appropriate tooling, and execute operations that yield accurate dimensions and surface finishes. Machinists work with a diverse range of materials, from metals to plastics, and they employ cutting-edge technology to achieve the desired results efficiently.

Being a machinist comes with a set of challenges due to the intricate nature of machining operations. Precision machining demands meticulous attention to detail, as even minor deviations can lead to components that are unusable or unsafe. Machinists must account for factors like tool wear, thermal expansion, and vibration, which can affect the accuracy of their work. Additionally, the programming and operation of CNC machines require a deep understanding of computer programming, machine dynamics, and tooling selection. The challenge lies in achieving perfection in dimensional accuracy, surface finish, and maintaining consistent quality across production runs.

The essence of being a machinist lies in the fulfillment derived from crafting objects with meticulous precision. Machinists witness the transformation of raw materials into intricate components, observing their work integrated into a variety of applications, from aerospace to medical devices. The moment a precisely machined part fits seamlessly into an assembly, contributing to the functionality of a larger system, is immensely gratifying. Machinists often experience a strong sense of accomplishment knowing that their craftsmanship directly impacts innovation and progress across industries. The tangible impact of their work fuels a deep sense of pride and a commitment to excellence.

Beyond the technical dimensions, being a machinist holds a unique significance in driving industrial progress and innovation. Machinists contribute to the development of cutting-edge technologies, manufacturing processes, and intricate components that power diverse sectors. Their work supports industries ranging from aerospace and automotive to electronics and medical equipment. Machinists are crucial to the production of precision parts that are integral to the functioning of everyday objects and complex machinery. Their role as precision craftsmen underscores their significance as enablers of innovation and progress, propelling society forward through the creation of meticulously crafted components.

In conclusion, being a machinist is a transformative journey that merges technical mastery, problem-solving skills, and a commitment to precision. Machinists are the architects of accuracy, shaping raw materials into components that drive innovation and progress across industries. The journey of a machinist is marked by a fascination with machinery, a dedication to precision craftsmanship, and the ability to navigate challenges inherent in precision machining. Challenges are met with adaptability, attention to detail, and an unwavering pursuit of perfection. The profound satisfaction of crafting components with accuracy, witnessing the tangible impact of their work, and contributing to innovation underscores the profound significance of the machinist's role. As machinists operate machinery and shape materials, they also shape the future, playing an indispensable role in industrial progress and technological advancement.

Unveiling Truths: Embarking on the Journey of a Journalist

Being a journalist is a transformative and influential endeavor that involves pursuing truth, disseminating information, and shaping public discourse. Journalists are the storytellers and watchdogs of society, responsible for gathering, investigating, and reporting news that informs, educates, and holds power to account. This section dives into the captivating world of being a journalist, exploring the motivations that drive individuals to pursue this demanding profession, the multifaceted roles journalists undertake, the challenges they confront in an ever-evolving media landscape, and the profound impact they wield in shaping the narratives that define our world.

Becoming a journalist often emerges from a sense of curiosity, a commitment to transparency, and a desire to empower individuals with information. Journalists are the conduits through which society learns about current events, social issues, and matters of public concern. The allure of the profession lies in the ability to ask probing questions, seek out facts, and convey stories that capture the essence of human experiences. Journalists often possess an innate sense of justice, an insatiable curiosity, and a passion for holding institutions accountable. The significance of journalism transcends its technical roles, as journalists serve as the guardians of democracy, promoting transparency and engaging citizens in informed decision-making.

The journey of a journalist is marked by the diversity of roles and responsibilities that extend beyond reporting. Journalists research, interview sources, write articles, and produce multimedia content across various platforms. They analyze complex issues, distill information, and present it in a clear, accessible manner. Journalists also serve as storytellers, giving voice to marginalized communities, shedding light on untold stories, and exposing injustices. In the digital age, journalists navigate a landscape of social media, video production, and data journalism, adapting their skills to engage audiences across different mediums. The versatility of journalism requires not only excellent communication skills but also a deep commitment to accuracy and ethical reporting.

Being a journalist comes with a set of challenges, particularly in an era of rapid technological advancements and the proliferation of misinformation. Journalists must navigate the delicate balance between speed and accuracy in reporting, ensuring that breaking news is delivered promptly without compromising the veracity of information. The rise of fake news and misinformation presents the challenge of distinguishing reliable sources from unreliable ones, and journalists must work to counteract misinformation with well-researched and fact-based reporting. Additionally, the challenges of censorship, threats to press freedom, and the erosion of trust in media require journalists to uphold their ethical responsibilities and maintain their commitment to holding power to account.

The essence of being a journalist lies in the profound impact that informed reporting can have on society. Journalists have the power to shape public opinion, drive social change, and expose issues that would otherwise remain hidden. The moment a news story prompts public awareness, sparks debate, or influences policy decisions is immensely gratifying for journalists. By uncovering realities, revealing injustices, and amplifying diverse voices, journalists contribute to a more informed and engaged citizenry. The ability to influence the course of events and contribute to positive change fuels a deep sense of purpose and dedication among journalists.

Beyond the technical aspects, being a journalist holds a unique significance in upholding democratic principles. Journalists play a vital role in fostering an informed citizenry, a cornerstone of democratic societies. They shine a light on government actions, corporate practices, and social issues, enabling citizens to make educated decisions. Journalists also serve as checks and balances, holding institutions accountable and ensuring that power is exercised responsibly. Their role as truth-seekers, storytellers, and advocates for transparency underscores their significance as pillars of democracy, promoting the open exchange of ideas and information that underpin free societies.

In conclusion, being a journalist is a transformative journey that blends passion for storytelling with a commitment to truth and accountability. Journalists are the narrators of society, tasked with unearthing facts, revealing stories, and shaping narratives that define our collective understanding. The journey of a journalist is marked by a thirst for knowledge, an unwavering commitment to ethical reporting, and the ability to navigate challenges in a rapidly evolving media landscape. Challenges are met with resilience, integrity, and a dedication to fostering an informed and engaged public. The profound satisfaction of illuminating realities, influencing public discourse, and shaping the course of events underscores the profound significance of the journalist's role. As journalists dig deeper, ask tough questions, and unveil truths, they illuminate the path to a more transparent, informed, and just society.

Justice and Judgment: Navigating the Role of a Judge

Being a judge is a profound and weighty responsibility that entails upholding the principles of justice, interpreting the law, and ensuring the fair administration of legal proceedings. Judges are the custodians of the legal system, presiding over cases, making rulings, and safeguarding the rights of individuals. This section explores into the intriguing world of being a judge, exploring the motivations that lead individuals to pursue this noble profession, the multifaceted roles judges undertake, the challenges they face in striking a balance between legal principles and societal dynamics, and the profound impact they wield in shaping the course of justice.

Becoming a judge often stems from a deep-rooted commitment to justice, a passion for upholding the rule of law, and a genuine desire to serve the community. Judges are the arbiters of fairness, ensuring that legal proceedings adhere to established norms and principles. The allure of the profession lies in the power to make decisions that influence the lives of individuals and the trajectory of legal precedent. Judges often possess a strong moral compass, a deep understanding of legal concepts, and the ability to apply impartiality in their judgments. The significance of being a judge extends beyond legal expertise, encompassing the responsibility to safeguard individual rights and uphold the integrity of the legal system.

The journey of a judge encompasses a range of roles that extend beyond presiding over cases. Judges interpret the law, analyze evidence, and apply legal principles to make informed decisions. They ensure that trials are conducted fairly, that parties are treated equitably, and that justice is served in alignment with legal norms. Judges also play a pivotal role in maintaining order in the courtroom, managing proceedings, and ensuring that due process is upheld. In appellate courts, judges review lower court decisions, analyze legal arguments, and contribute to the development of legal precedents. The multifaceted nature of the judge's role demands not only legal acumen but also a deep sense of integrity and ethical conduct.

Being a judge presents a unique set of challenges, largely due to the complexities of legal cases, the diverse array of individuals involved, and the evolving nature of societal dynamics. Judges must remain impartial and objective, despite potential personal biases, ensuring that justice is served without favoritism. The challenge lies in making decisions that balance legal precedent with the need to adapt to changing norms and values. Moreover, the emotional weight of cases, especially those involving sensitive issues, demands a high level of emotional intelligence and resilience. Judges must also navigate the pressures of public scrutiny, ensuring that their decisions are guided solely by the law and not influenced by external factors.

The essence of being a judge lies in the impact that their decisions have on individuals, society, and the legal system as a whole. Judges play a critical role in ensuring that individuals' rights are protected, that legal norms are upheld, and that justice is served. The moment a judge renders a verdict, delivering closure to litigants, setting a legal precedent, or contributing to the evolution of legal principles, is immensely powerful. The ability to shape legal outcomes, influence societal norms, and safeguard individual liberties fuels a sense of purpose and dedication among judges. Their work contributes to the maintenance of a just and equitable society and ensures that the rule of law remains a cornerstone of democratic governance.

Beyond the technical aspects, being a judge carries a unique significance in upholding democratic principles and due process. Judges are essential in ensuring that laws are applied fairly and that individual rights are protected from infringement. They serve as a check on government actions, preventing abuse of power and upholding the balance of the three branches of government. Judges also contribute to legal education by clarifying legal standards, resolving legal disputes, and contributing to the development of jurisprudence. Their role as impartial interpreters and guardians of the legal system underscores their significance as pillars of democratic governance and protectors of individual rights.

In conclusion, being a judge is a transformative journey that merges legal expertise with a commitment to justice and fairness. Judges are the guardians of the legal system, responsible for interpreting laws, resolving disputes, and upholding the principles of democracy. The journey of a judge is marked by a dedication to fairness, an unwavering commitment to the rule of law, and the ability to navigate challenges in an ever-changing legal landscape. Challenges are met with integrity, impartiality, and a deep sense of responsibility to serve society. The profound impact of their decisions on individual lives, legal precedent, and the course of justice underscores the profound significance of the judge's role. As judges uphold justice, interpret laws, and safeguard rights, they also uphold the foundations of democratic governance, ensuring that the legal system remains a beacon of fairness and accountability.

Mastering Financial Alchemy: Navigating the World of Investment Banking

Being an investment banker is a dynamic and influential role that involves facilitating financial transactions, advising clients, and driving economic growth. Investment bankers are financial experts who work at the forefront of capital markets, connecting businesses with investors and offering strategic financial guidance. This section adventures into the captivating world of being an investment banker, exploring the motivations that lead individuals to pursue this demanding profession, the multifaceted roles they undertake, the challenges faced in navigating complex financial landscapes, and the profound impact they wield in shaping economic structures.

Becoming an investment banker often stems from a fascination with finance, a knack for strategic thinking, and a desire to drive financial success for both clients and institutions. Investment bankers serve as intermediaries, helping companies raise capital, execute mergers and acquisitions, and navigate intricate financial transactions. The allure of the profession lies in the ability to harness financial tools and strategies to create value and foster growth. Investment bankers often possess a deep understanding of market dynamics, a talent for structuring complex deals, and an affinity for balancing risk and reward. The significance of investment banking extends beyond financial expertise, encompassing the role of shaping corporate strategies and influencing economic landscapes.

The journey of an investment banker encompasses a wide array of roles that extend beyond traditional financial analysis. Investment bankers work as advisors, providing strategic insights to clients on matters such as capital raising, restructuring, and expansion. They engage in due diligence, analyzing financial data to assess the viability of investments and transactions. Investment bankers also manage relationships with clients and investors, ensuring that their financial objectives are aligned with market trends. In addition, investment bankers engage in market research, staying informed about industry trends, economic indicators, and regulatory changes that impact financial decisions. The multifaceted nature of the investment banker's role demands not only financial acumen but also effective communication and negotiation skills.

Being an investment banker presents a unique set of challenges, largely due to the complexities of global markets, the volatility of economic conditions, and the ever-evolving regulatory landscape. Investment bankers must navigate intricate financial structures, assess risks, and create strategies that optimize returns. They face challenges in accurately forecasting market trends, managing the uncertainties of financial markets, and responding swiftly to changes in economic conditions. Additionally, investment bankers must ensure compliance with legal and regulatory requirements, which can vary across jurisdictions. The challenge lies in the ability to make informed decisions in high-pressure environments, adapt to rapid changes, and balance the interests of diverse stakeholders.

The essence of being an investment banker lies in the profound impact they have on businesses, economies, and financial systems. Investment bankers play a pivotal role in facilitating transactions that drive growth, support innovation, and create jobs. The moment a successful capital raising effort enables a company to expand its operations, or a well-executed merger enhances market competitiveness, underscores the significance of investment bankers' work. By orchestrating financial deals that fuel economic progress, investment bankers contribute to shaping industries, stimulating innovation, and fostering global economic growth. Their ability to assess financial landscapes, devise strategic plans, and drive transactions with precision fuels a sense of purpose and responsibility.

Beyond the technical aspects, being an investment banker carries a unique significance in shaping the structure of financial markets and influencing economic dynamics. Investment bankers contribute to the development of financial products and strategies that reshape market trends and investment opportunities. They play a role in driving sustainable finance, promoting responsible investing, and aligning financial decisions with environmental and social considerations. Investment bankers also act as economic navigators, offering insights that guide businesses and investors through economic uncertainties. Their role as financial pioneers and advisors underscores their significance as architects of economic progress and stewards of responsible finance.

In conclusion, being an investment banker is a transformative journey that merges financial expertise with a commitment to driving economic growth and success. Investment bankers are financial visionaries, orchestrating transactions that shape industries, support businesses, and drive global economic progress. The journey of an investment banker is marked by a passion for finance, a dedication to strategic thinking, and the ability to navigate challenges in complex financial landscapes. Challenges are met with adaptability, market insights, and a relentless pursuit of value creation. The profound impact of their work on corporate strategies, economic structures, and market trends underscores the profound significance of the investment banker's role. As investment bankers forge financial paths, structure deals, and drive economic growth, they stand as financial architects and economic enablers who shape the trajectory of industries and economies alike.

Balancing Books and Beyond:
The Accountant's Odyssey

Accountants, the financial navigators of the business world, play a crucial role in maintaining the financial health of organizations. With their meticulous attention to detail, analytical prowess, and ethical commitment, they ensure that financial records are accurate, transparent, and compliant. This section delves into the realm of an accountant, exploring the significance of their role, the diverse responsibilities they undertake, the skills they cultivate, the challenges they confront, and the satisfaction derived from guiding businesses toward fiscal stability.

Accountants are more than mere number-crunchers; they are the custodians of financial integrity. They contribute to informed decision-making, regulatory compliance, and strategic planning. Accountants help businesses optimize their financial resources, enhance operational efficiency, and adapt to changing economic landscapes. Moreover, their work is essential for ensuring accountability, transparency, and ethical practices in financial reporting.

The responsibilities of an accountant span a wide spectrum, from maintaining ledgers to providing strategic financial insights. Accountants track financial transactions, create financial statements, and ensure compliance with accounting standards and tax regulations. They analyze financial data to identify trends, opportunities, and areas that require attention. Accountants also play a critical role in budgeting, forecasting, and advising management on financial strategies that align with the organization's goals.

Being a successful accountant demands a combination of technical expertise and analytical finesse. Accountants must possess a deep understanding of accounting principles, financial reporting, and tax laws to accurately record and interpret financial data. Proficiency in using accounting software and advanced spreadsheet tools is essential for efficient data analysis. Strong attention to detail is crucial to identifying discrepancies and ensuring the accuracy of financial records. Moreover, analytical skills enable accountants to extract meaningful insights from data, supporting informed business decisions.

The life of an accountant comes with its own set of challenges. The meticulous nature of accounting work demands precision, leaving little room for error. Navigating complex tax codes and regulations can be daunting, requiring accountants to stay updated with changes in the legal landscape. The pressure of meeting deadlines, especially during tax seasons or fiscal year-end, can be stressful. However, the rewards are substantial. The satisfaction of reconciling financial discrepancies, ensuring financial compliance, and contributing to organizational success is deeply gratifying. Moreover, the stable career prospects, diverse industry opportunities, and potential for growth within finance and management roles make being an accountant a fulfilling choice.

In conclusion, being an accountant is a dynamic journey that blends financial expertise with strategic insights. Accountants are the architects of fiscal stability, providing businesses with the foundation for informed decision-making and sustainable growth. Their influence extends beyond numbers; they contribute to ethical financial practices, regulatory compliance, and financial transparency. Despite the challenges, the rewards of seeing financial order emerge from complexity, offering strategic counsel, and being a catalyst for organizational success make being an accountant a highly impactful and rewarding profession. Accountants are the silent partners in businesses, embodying the pursuit of financial excellence and ethical integrity that underpins economic progress.

Digging Through Time: Exploring the Past as an Archaeologist

Archaeologists, the modern-day explorers of the past, delve deep into the earth to uncover the remnants of civilizations that have long faded into history. With their meticulous excavations, analytical acumen, and reverence for heritage, they piece together narratives that bridge the gap between the ancient and the present. This section dives into the realm of an archaeologist, exploring the significance of their role, the diverse responsibilities they shoulder, the skills they refine, the challenges they confront, and the sense of discovery that accompanies those who unearth the mysteries of the past.

Archaeologists play a pivotal role in preserving humanity's cultural heritage and understanding the trajectory of human evolution. They uncover artifacts, structures, and even entire cities that offer insights into the lifestyles, technologies, and belief systems of ancient civilizations. Archaeologists contribute to rewriting history, illuminating forgotten chapters, and challenging preconceived notions. Beyond the academic realm, their work has cultural, social, and economic implications, fostering appreciation for diverse cultures and attracting tourists to historical sites.

The responsibilities of an archaeologist encompass a wide range of activities, from excavations to research and preservation. Archaeologists plan and execute excavations, carefully removing layers of soil to reveal artifacts and structures without damaging them. They analyze the recovered artifacts, documenting their context, materials, and functions. Archaeologists also conduct research, interpret findings, and contribute to scholarly publications. Preservation is a critical aspect, involving strategies to safeguard excavated materials, protect sites from deterioration, and educate the public about their historical significance.

Being a successful archaeologist demands a unique blend of fieldwork, analytical thinking, and interdisciplinary knowledge. Archaeologists must have a deep understanding of archaeological methods, stratigraphy, and chronology to accurately interpret findings. They refine skills in artifact identification, analysis of ancient technologies, and deciphering ancient scripts or languages. Proficiency in scientific techniques, such as radiocarbon dating or DNA analysis, enhances their ability to date artifacts and reconstruct ancient lives. Additionally, effective communication skills are vital for presenting findings to both scholarly and public audiences.

The life of an archaeologist is not without its challenges. Fieldwork often involves physically demanding conditions, ranging from extreme climates to challenging terrains. The meticulous nature of excavations requires patience and attention to detail. Preservation efforts demand innovative solutions to counteract deterioration due to weather, pollution, or human impact. Moreover, competition for funding and academic positions can be fierce. However, the rewards are profound. The thrill of discovery, the satisfaction of contributing to historical knowledge, and the chance to immerse oneself in cultures long past create a sense of purpose and fulfillment unique to the profession.

In conclusion, being an archaeologist is a journey that transcends time, merging exploration, research, and preservation. Archaeologists are the storytellers of civilizations, uncovering fragments of the past to reconstruct the intricate tapestry of human history. Their significance goes beyond academia, influencing cultural appreciation, identity, and global heritage. Despite the challenges, the rewards of unearthing artifacts, unraveling mysteries, and reimagining past societies provide archaeologists with a deep sense of purpose. Archaeologists stand as stewards of time, embodying the quest for knowledge, the reverence for history, and the dedication to preserving the echoes of those who came before us.

Exploring the Mind: Navigating the Pathways of Being a Psychologist

Being a psychologist is a transformative and empathetic journey that involves understanding human behavior, providing therapeutic support, and contributing to mental well-being. Psychologists are experts in the realm of the mind, utilizing their knowledge to help individuals navigate challenges, overcome obstacles, and achieve personal growth. This section dives into the captivating world of being a psychologist, exploring the motivations that drive individuals to enter this meaningful profession, the diverse roles psychologists undertake, the challenges they face in unraveling the complexities of human psychology, and the profound impact they have on fostering emotional resilience and psychological healing.

Becoming a psychologist often arises from a deep compassion for others, a fascination with the intricacies of human behavior, and a desire to make a positive impact on mental health. Psychologists serve as guides, offering support to individuals facing a wide range of emotional, cognitive, and behavioral challenges. The allure of the profession lies in the opportunity to help people confront their struggles, develop coping strategies, and achieve mental well-being. Psychologists often possess a keen ability to empathize, a genuine desire to facilitate personal growth, and a strong belief in the transformative power of therapy. The significance of psychology extends beyond therapeutic skills, encompassing the role of advocates for mental health awareness and emotional resilience.

The journey of a psychologist encompasses an array of roles that extend beyond individual therapy. Psychologists work as clinicians, conducting assessments, diagnosing mental health conditions, and creating personalized treatment plans. They also engage in research, contributing to the understanding of human behavior, cognition, and emotions. Psychologists serve as educators, disseminating knowledge about psychological well-being and promoting healthy coping mechanisms. Additionally, psychologists work in diverse settings, including schools, hospitals, corporations, and prisons, addressing a wide spectrum of psychological needs. The multifaceted nature of the psychologist's role demands not only clinical skills but also strong communication and cultural sensitivity.

Being a psychologist presents a unique set of challenges due to the complexities of the human psyche and the varied nature of mental health concerns. Psychologists must navigate the delicate balance of establishing trust, respecting confidentiality, and fostering a therapeutic alliance with their clients. They work with individuals facing a range of issues, from anxiety and depression to trauma and personality disorders, each requiring a tailored approach. The challenge lies in assessing the underlying causes of psychological distress, identifying effective interventions, and promoting sustainable emotional well-being. Additionally, psychologists must address cultural and ethical considerations to ensure that their interventions are culturally sensitive and ethically sound.

The essence of being a psychologist lies in the healing impact they have on individuals and communities. Psychologists witness the transformation of clients as they confront their challenges, develop self-awareness, and acquire tools to manage their mental health. The moment a client experiences a breakthrough, learns healthy coping strategies, or develops insights that lead to personal growth, underscores the significance of the psychologist's work. By providing a safe space for self-expression, offering guidance, and promoting emotional resilience, psychologists contribute to fostering mental health and well-being. The ability to witness positive change, empower individuals, and alleviate psychological distress fuels a deep sense of fulfillment and purpose.

Beyond the clinical aspects, being a psychologist holds a unique significance in promoting mental health awareness and resilience on a societal level. Psychologists contribute to destigmatizing mental health issues, raising awareness about the importance of seeking help, and fostering a culture of emotional well-being. They play a role in designing and implementing interventions that address psychological challenges in schools, workplaces, and communities. Additionally, psychologists contribute to the broader understanding of human behavior, informing public policies and social initiatives that support mental health. Their role as advocates for psychological well-being underscores their significance as agents of positive change in society.

In conclusion, being a psychologist is a transformative journey that merges compassion with scientific knowledge, contributing to the emotional well-being and growth of individuals and communities. Psychologists are healers of the mind, guiding individuals through challenges, facilitating personal insights, and fostering emotional resilience. The journey of a psychologist is marked by empathy, a commitment to understanding human behavior, and the ability to navigate challenges in a dynamic field. Challenges are met with adaptability, cultural sensitivity, and a deep sense of ethical responsibility. The profound impact of their work on promoting mental health, fostering emotional well-being, and supporting personal growth underscores the profound significance of the psychologist's role. As psychologists unravel minds, offer support, and empower individuals to lead healthier lives, they stand as beacons of compassion and advocates for emotional resilience in a complex world.

Unlocking Minds: The Journey
of a Psychiatrist

Psychiatrists, the healers of the mind, embark on a profound journey that explores into the complexities of human thoughts, emotions, and behaviors. Armed with medical expertise, empathetic understanding, and therapeutic techniques, they address a wide range of mental health challenges. This section adventures into the world of a psychiatrist, exploring the significance of their role, the diverse responsibilities they shoulder, the skills they cultivate, the challenges they confront, and the deep satisfaction they derive from nurturing mental well-being and improving the lives of their patients.

Psychiatrists hold a pivotal role in the realm of healthcare, as they focus on diagnosing, treating, and preventing mental illnesses. They play a critical part in enhancing individuals' quality of life by addressing disorders that impact cognitive, emotional, and behavioral facets. Psychiatrists serve as advocates for mental health awareness, challenging stigma, and providing comprehensive care that considers the intricate interplay between biological, psychological, and social factors.

The responsibilities of a psychiatrist encompass a broad array of tasks, from conducting patient assessments and diagnosing conditions to implementing treatment plans and offering therapeutic interventions. Psychiatrists engage in comprehensive evaluations to understand patients' medical history, current symptoms, and psychological needs. They prescribe medications, administer psychotherapy sessions, and collaborate with other healthcare professionals to ensure holistic care. Psychiatrists also provide guidance on lifestyle changes and coping strategies that empower patients to manage their mental health.

Being a successful psychiatrist requires a blend of medical knowledge, psychological insight, and compassionate communication. Psychiatrists must possess an in-depth understanding of human psychology, psychopathology, and the intricacies of mental disorders. Proficiency in therapeutic techniques, such as cognitive-behavioral therapy, dialectical behavior therapy, and psychoanalysis, is essential. Effective communication skills are crucial for establishing rapport with patients, creating a safe space for self-expression, and facilitating meaningful therapeutic relationships.

The life of a psychiatrist is marked by both challenges and rewards. Diagnosing mental disorders requires careful consideration of symptoms, as well as differentiating between various conditions that may present similarly. Building trust with patients and encouraging them to openly discuss their feelings can be challenging, especially given the stigma surrounding mental health. Moreover, psychiatrists need to stay updated with the evolving field of psychiatry and its treatments. However, the rewards are profound. The satisfaction of witnessing patients' personal growth, the alleviation of their distress, and the restoration of their mental well-being is deeply gratifying. The ability to make a lasting impact on individuals' lives through compassionate care and tailored interventions is the driving force behind this profession.

In conclusion, being a psychiatrist is a transformative journey that merges medical knowledge with empathetic care. Psychiatrists stand as champions of mental health, promoting well-being, diagnosing conditions, and empowering individuals to lead fulfilling lives. Their influence extends beyond treating mental disorders; they challenge stigma, provide solace, and foster resilience. Despite the challenges, the rewards of nurturing mental wellness, witnessing patients' progress, and facilitating personal growth make being a psychiatrist an exceptionally fulfilling career. Psychiatrists stand as advocates for mental health, embodying the commitment to understanding, compassion, and the profound impact of mental well-being on the human experience.

Forecasting the Elements:
Navigating the Science and Wonders
of Being a Meteorologist

Being a meteorologist is an intriguing and essential pursuit that involves studying the Earth's atmosphere, predicting weather patterns, and safeguarding communities from the impacts of natural phenomena. Meteorologists are experts in the science of weather and climate, utilizing their knowledge to provide accurate forecasts, analyze atmospheric data, and contribute to our understanding of the Earth's dynamic systems. This section delves into the captivating world of being a meteorologist, exploring the motivations that drive individuals to pursue this scientifically rich profession, the multifaceted roles they undertake, the challenges they face in decoding complex weather phenomena, and the profound impact they have on societal preparedness and environmental awareness.

Becoming a meteorologist often originates from a deep curiosity about the natural world, a fascination with weather patterns, and a desire to contribute to public safety. Meteorologists are the guardians of weather knowledge, interpreting atmospheric data to provide forecasts and inform decision-making. The allure of the profession lies in the ability to decode the intricacies of the Earth's systems, predict weather events, and disseminate vital information to individuals and communities. Meteorologists possess a passion for scientific inquiry, an affinity for analyzing data, and a commitment to translating complex concepts into actionable insights. The significance of meteorology extends beyond forecasting; it encompasses the role of environmental stewards who contribute to climate awareness and disaster preparedness.

The journey of a meteorologist encompasses a range of roles that extend beyond weather prediction. Meteorologists work as researchers, conducting studies to enhance our understanding of climate patterns, atmospheric dynamics, and the impact of climate change. They engage in data analysis, utilizing advanced technologies to interpret meteorological information and develop predictive models. Meteorologists also communicate with the public, providing weather forecasts and warnings to ensure the safety of individuals in the face of severe weather events. Additionally, meteorologists contribute to public policy, offering insights into climate-related issues that impact industries, agriculture, and urban planning. The multifaceted nature of the meteorologist's role demands not only scientific expertise but also effective communication and public engagement skills.

Being a meteorologist presents a unique set of challenges due to the intricate and dynamic nature of atmospheric processes. Meteorologists must interpret vast amounts of data from various sources, including satellites, weather stations, and computer models, to develop accurate forecasts. They must navigate uncertainties in weather prediction, address the limitations of current technology, and account for rapid changes in atmospheric conditions. The challenge lies in deciphering complex weather patterns, predicting severe weather events, and communicating potential hazards effectively to the public. Meteorologists must also tackle the broader challenge of understanding climate change, its causes, and potential impacts on the planet.

The essence of being a meteorologist lies in the impact they have on public safety, disaster preparedness, and climate education. Meteorologists play a pivotal role in forecasting severe weather events, such as hurricanes, tornadoes, and blizzards, allowing communities to take proactive measures to minimize damage and protect lives. The moment a well-timed weather warning enables individuals to evacuate an area or take shelter during a storm highlights the significance of meteorologists' work. By educating the public about weather phenomena, raising climate awareness, and providing valuable information to industries, meteorologists contribute to fostering resilient communities and promoting sustainable practices.

Beyond the scientific aspects, being a meteorologist holds a unique significance in fostering environmental awareness and advocating for sustainable practices. Meteorologists contribute to the broader understanding of climate change, the impact of human activities on the environment, and the need for responsible stewardship of natural resources. They play a role in raising awareness about the interconnectedness of weather patterns, ecosystems, and human activities. Meteorologists also contribute to research initiatives that inform policies addressing climate-related challenges. Their role as communicators, educators, and advocates for environmental consciousness underscores their significance as agents of positive change in addressing global environmental issues.

In conclusion, being a meteorologist is a transformative journey that merges scientific inquiry with a commitment to public safety, environmental awareness, and climate education. Meteorologists are the interpreters of atmospheric dynamics, translating complex data into actionable insights for individuals and communities. The journey of a meteorologist is marked by curiosity, a dedication to scientific exploration, and the ability to navigate challenges in decoding the mysteries of the Earth's systems. Challenges are met with data analysis, technological innovation, and a deep commitment to promoting safety and environmental consciousness. The profound impact of their work on weather prediction, disaster preparedness, and climate education underscores the profound significance of the meteorologist's role. As meteorologists decode atmospheric puzzles, offer critical insights, and contribute to climate awareness, they stand as stewards of environmental well-being and guardians of the safety of societies worldwide.

Exploring Life's Diversity: Embarking on the Journey of a Biologist

Being a biologist is a captivating and enlightening pursuit that involves the study of life in all its intricate forms, from microscopic organisms to complex ecosystems. Biologists are scientists who unravel the mysteries of existence, exploring the mechanisms of life, conducting research, and contributing to our understanding of the natural world. This section dives into the fascinating realm of being a biologist, exploring the motivations that drive individuals to embark on this journey, the diverse roles biologists undertake, the challenges they encounter in deciphering life's complexities, and the profound impact they have on scientific progress, conservation, and our collective knowledge.

Becoming a biologist often arises from a profound curiosity about the natural world, a fascination with living organisms, and a desire to uncover the secrets of life's diversity. Biologists are the observers of nature's intricacies, conducting research to understand the fundamental processes that govern life. The allure of the profession lies in the opportunity to explore uncharted territories, from the mysteries of genetics to the intricacies of ecosystems. Biologists possess a natural inquisitiveness, a passion for experimentation, and an affinity for understanding how life adapts and evolves. The significance of biology extends beyond scientific inquiry; it encompasses the role of stewards of biodiversity and advocates for conservation.

The journey of a biologist encompasses a range of roles that extend beyond laboratory research. Biologists work as researchers, investigating biological phenomena, conducting experiments, and advancing our understanding of life's mechanisms. They engage in fieldwork, studying ecosystems, species interactions, and environmental changes. Biologists also play a role in education, sharing their knowledge with students, and contributing to public awareness about the importance of biodiversity and environmental sustainability. Additionally, biologists work in various sectors, including medicine, agriculture, and conservation, addressing a wide spectrum of biological challenges. The multifaceted nature of the biologist's role demands not only scientific expertise but also effective communication and interdisciplinary collaboration.

Being a biologist presents a unique set of challenges due to the intricacies of life's interconnected systems and the vastness of biological diversity. Biologists must navigate the complexities of genetic interactions, ecological relationships, and the impact of human activities on ecosystems. They face challenges in gathering accurate data, designing experiments, and interpreting results that can inform scientific knowledge and guide conservation efforts. The challenge lies in deciphering the mechanisms of life, identifying species, understanding ecological balance, and unraveling the implications of environmental changes. Biologists must also address ethical considerations, ensuring that their research and interventions prioritize the well-being of ecosystems and species.

The essence of being a biologist lies in the impact they have on scientific progress, environmental conservation, and our collective knowledge of life's intricacies. Biologists contribute to groundbreaking discoveries that expand our understanding of genetics, evolution, and ecology. The moment a new species is identified, a novel mechanism is uncovered, or a scientific breakthrough is achieved highlights the significance of biologists' work. By studying ecosystems, tracking species populations, and advocating for conservation, biologists contribute to preserving biodiversity, protecting endangered species, and promoting sustainable land and resource management. Their ability to advance scientific knowledge and safeguard the natural world fuels a deep sense of purpose and responsibility.

Beyond the scientific dimensions, being a biologist carries a unique significance in advancing human understanding of life and advocating for environmental stewardship. Biologists contribute to our broader awareness of the interconnectedness of species, ecosystems, and the environment. They play a role in addressing global challenges such as climate change, habitat loss, and emerging diseases. Biologists also foster public awareness about the importance of biodiversity, inspiring individuals to connect with nature and participate in conservation efforts. Their role as catalysts of scientific discovery and guardians of nature underscores their significance as agents of positive change in shaping a sustainable and harmonious relationship between humans and the natural world.

In conclusion, being a biologist is a transformative journey that merges scientific inquiry with a commitment to understanding life's intricacies and advocating for its conservation. Biologists are explorers of the living world, uncovering the mechanisms of existence, studying ecosystems, and contributing to our understanding of biodiversity. The journey of a biologist is marked by curiosity, a dedication to discovery, and the ability to navigate challenges in decoding life's mysteries. Challenges are met with scientific rigor, data analysis, and a deep sense of responsibility for the well-being of species and ecosystems. The profound impact of their work on scientific progress, conservation efforts, and environmental awareness underscores the profound significance of the biologist's role. As biologists delve into the complexity of life, uncover its secrets, and champion its preservation, they stand as advocates for nature's wonders and guardians of the delicate balance of the natural world.

Reactions Unveiled: A Chemist's Journey Through Matter Transformations

Chemistry, often referred to as the "central science," stands as a fascinating discipline that explores into the profound intricacies of matter, its properties, and transformations. As a chemist, one becomes a modern-day alchemist, deciphering the mysteries of the atomic and molecular realm. This section embarks on a journey through the world of a chemist, highlighting the significance of chemistry, the role of a chemist in society, the scientific process involved, the challenges faced, and the rewards reaped.

Chemistry is the driving force behind the transformation of raw elements into compounds that shape our daily lives. From the materials that construct our world to the medicines that heal our bodies, chemistry's impact is ubiquitous. Chemists lay the groundwork for technological innovations, enabling advancements in fields such as energy production, materials science, and pharmaceuticals. By understanding the composition and behavior of substances, chemists contribute to solving global challenges like climate change and resource depletion.

Chemists are the architects of matter. They design experiments to unveil the secrets hidden within compounds and develop new materials that propel industries forward. Analytical chemists decipher the composition of substances, while organic chemists synthesize novel compounds. Physical chemists explore the fundamental principles governing reactions, and biochemists delve into the molecular mechanisms of life. Environmental chemists address pollution concerns, and medicinal chemists craft remedies for ailments. Through their multidisciplinary efforts, chemists contribute indispensably to scientific progress.

The chemist's journey begins with curiosity. Research questions are formulated, hypotheses are constructed, and experiments are designed. Observations are made, data is collected, and patterns emerge. Through meticulous analysis, chemists uncover underlying principles and draw connections. The scientific method guides their approach, ensuring objectivity and reliability. Collaboration is also crucial, as chemists often work in teams to tackle complex challenges that require diverse expertise. This process culminates in the dissemination of findings through publications, contributing to the collective knowledge of the field.

The path of a chemist is not without obstacles. Experiments may fail, hypotheses may be disproven, and setbacks may arise. The precision demanded by chemistry requires patience and resilience. The quest for new knowledge is often accompanied by ethical considerations, especially in fields like pharmaceuticals and environmental chemistry. However, the rewards of a chemist's journey are immeasurable. The thrill of discovery, the satisfaction of solving puzzles on a molecular level, and the potential to make transformative contributions to society are deeply gratifying.

In conclusion, being a chemist is a captivating and purposeful pursuit that explores the essence of matter and its transformations. Chemists play an essential role in shaping our understanding of the natural world and in forging advancements that impact society on a global scale. Through a systematic scientific process, chemists unlock the secrets of matter, addressing challenges and uncovering opportunities. The journey of a chemist is both intellectually stimulating and socially impactful, underscoring the vital role that chemistry plays in our lives.

Exploring the Quantum Universe: A Physicist's Odyssey Through Space, Time, and Fundamental Forces

Physics, the fundamental science that seeks to comprehend the intricacies of the universe, stands as a beacon of human curiosity and exploration. Physicists are the modern-day adventurers who venture into the realms of the unimaginably small and the unfathomably large, unraveling the secrets that govern the cosmos. This section adventures into the world of a physicist, shedding light on the significance of physics, the multifaceted roles physicists play, the scientific methodology they employ, the challenges they face, and the profound rewards that come from understanding the universe at its core.

Physics is the cornerstone of natural science, serving as the foundation upon which other scientific disciplines are built. It explores the fundamental principles that underlie the behavior of matter, energy, space, and time. From the tiniest subatomic particles to the vastness of cosmic structures, physics strives to provide a comprehensive framework for understanding the universe. It has led to technological marvels that shape our modern world, from electricity and magnetism to the theories behind the internet and space exploration.

Physicists assume an array of roles, each contributing to our expanding knowledge of the universe. Theoretical physicists engage in abstract thought experiments and mathematical modeling to formulate groundbreaking theories, while experimental physicists design and conduct intricate experiments to test these theories against the tangible world. Astrophysicists gaze at distant stars and galaxies, seeking to unlock the mysteries of the cosmos, while particle physicists collide particles at incredibly high energies to probe the very building blocks of matter. Interdisciplinary collaborations enable physicists to contribute to fields like engineering, medicine, and environmental science.

The journey of a physicist commences with curiosity and a question. A hypothesis is crafted, and experiments or calculations are designed to test its validity. Data is meticulously collected and analyzed, revealing patterns and anomalies that hint at underlying truths. The scientific method guides physicists in their pursuit of empirical evidence, fostering objectivity and rigor. Mathematical language becomes a powerful tool to describe the intricate relationships and phenomena that shape the universe. Peer review and collaboration ensure the reliability of findings, as knowledge advances collectively.

The path of a physicist is not devoid of challenges. The questions posed are often complex, requiring innovative approaches and novel methodologies. The pursuit of knowledge may lead to dead ends, and the language of mathematics can be an insurmountable barrier for some. Additionally, grappling with the unknown can be intellectually and emotionally demanding. Yet, the rewards of being a physicist are profound. The thrill of discovery, the satisfaction of contributing to our understanding of reality, and the potential to inspire future generations are deeply gratifying.

In conclusion, being a physicist is a captivating journey that embodies humanity's insatiable quest for understanding. Physicists serve as the explorers of the unknown, illuminating the mysteries that shape our existence. From deciphering the behavior of particles at the subatomic scale to unraveling the vast cosmic tapestry, physicists wield their intellectual prowess to transform abstract theories into tangible insights. The challenges they face are met with resilience and determination, rewarded by the boundless joy of discovery and the privilege of advancing human knowledge. The pursuit of physics transcends time and culture, uniting us in the universal endeavor to unravel the enigmas that define our reality.

Unearthing Earth's Story:
A Geologist's Expedition
Through Time and Terrain

Geology, the scientific study of Earth's structure, composition, and history, is a captivating discipline that grants geologists a unique insight into the planet's evolution over billions of years. Geologists are modern-day detectives, piecing together the puzzle of Earth's past and present to understand its intricate workings. This section delves into the world of a geologist, exploring the importance of geology, the diverse roles geologists play, the scientific approaches they employ, the challenges they encounter, and the gratifying rewards that stem from unlocking the Earth's secrets.

Geology is the foundation upon which our understanding of Earth is built. It not only reveals the processes that have shaped our planet's surface, but also provides invaluable information about its resources, hazards, and potential for sustainable development. Geologists contribute to addressing critical issues such as climate change, natural disasters, and resource management. By deciphering the past, geologists help us prepare for the future and make informed decisions that affect both humanity and the environment.

Geologists take on multifaceted roles that extend far beyond mere rock collection. They may specialize in various subfields such as mineralogy, petrology, paleontology, or structural geology. Exploration geologists locate valuable minerals and resources, while environmental geologists assess the impact of human activities on the planet. Stratigraphers unravel Earth's history through layers of sediment, and geomorphologists study the processes that shape landforms. Geologists also contribute to energy exploration, engineering projects, and policy-making, showcasing the diversity and versatility of their expertise.

The journey of a geologist begins with keen observation. Whether in the field, examining rock formations, or in the laboratory, analyzing mineral samples, observation is the foundation of geologic inquiry. Geologists employ a combination of fieldwork, laboratory analysis, and advanced technology to collect and interpret data. They reconstruct ancient environments, interpret seismic activity, and study the movement of Earth's tectonic plates. Collaboration is pivotal, as geologists often collaborate across disciplines to form a comprehensive understanding of Earth's processes.

Being a geologist comes with unique challenges. Fieldwork can be physically demanding, taking geologists to remote and often harsh environments. Analyzing complex geological structures requires patience and attention to detail. Additionally, predicting natural disasters and mitigating their impact involves a significant responsibility. However, the rewards of being a geologist are both intellectually fulfilling and socially impactful. The thrill of making groundbreaking discoveries, contributing to our understanding of Earth's history, and safeguarding communities from geological hazards are deeply rewarding aspects of the profession.

In conclusion, being a geologist is an enriching journey that allows one to unravel the mysteries of our planet and contribute to its sustainable future. Geologists serve as custodians of Earth's history, helping us decipher the stories embedded within its rocks and landscapes. Their work extends from the microscopic scale of minerals to the grand scale of tectonic movements, demonstrating the breadth and depth of their explorations. The challenges they face are met with determination, and the rewards they reap are both personal and societal. As stewards of Earth's past, present, and future, geologists play a vital role in preserving the planet for generations to come.

Stargazing through Time:
An Astronomer's Odyssey
Across the Cosmos

Astronomy, the awe-inspiring study of the cosmos beyond our world, beckons astronomers to peer into the vast expanse of space and time. Astronomers are the modern explorers who journey through the universe, unraveling its mysteries and expanding our understanding of the cosmos. This section dives into the realm of an astronomer, highlighting the significance of astronomy, the multifaceted roles astronomers play, the methods they employ to unravel cosmic enigmas, the challenges they face, and the profound revelations that come from gazing at the stars.

Astronomy holds a special place as one of the oldest natural sciences, tracing back to humanity's early curiosity about the heavens. It extends our reach beyond Earth's boundaries, allowing us to comprehend the universe's origins, its structure, and its evolution. Astronomical discoveries have not only reshaped our understanding of our place in the cosmos but also led to technological advancements that impact our daily lives, from GPS navigation to medical imaging techniques.

Astronomers don various roles, reflecting the multifaceted nature of their field. Observational astronomers utilize powerful telescopes to capture distant light, unveiling the properties of stars, galaxies, and other celestial bodies. Theoretical astronomers employ complex mathematical models to decipher the underlying laws governing the universe's behavior. Astrobiologists explore the possibility of life beyond Earth, while cosmologists probe the universe's origin and fate. Public outreach and education are also integral, as astronomers inspire and engage the public in the wonders of the cosmos.

The journey of an astronomer often commences with gazing at the night sky, armed with telescopes or sophisticated observatories. Observational data is collected, ranging from the faintest light of distant galaxies to the energetic emissions of pulsars and black holes. Analysis involves data processing, statistical methods, and advanced simulations to decipher the cosmos' intricate language. Astronomy is a collaborative endeavor, where international teams share data, insights, and theories, leading to a collective understanding of the universe's secrets.

The life of an astronomer is not without challenges. Securing observation time on advanced telescopes can be competitive, and adverse weather conditions can impede data collection. Analyzing complex data sets requires a strong background in mathematics and computer programming. Additionally, grappling with the vastness of the universe and the limitations of human understanding can be intellectually humbling. However, the rewards of being an astronomer are deeply fulfilling. The thrill of discovering new celestial phenomena, the satisfaction of contributing to fundamental scientific knowledge, and the ability to inspire wonder and curiosity in others are among the many gratifying aspects.

In conclusion, being an astronomer is an incredible voyage that takes one beyond Earth's confines to explore the universe's grand tapestry. Astronomers peer into the heavens to decipher its language, uncover its history, and discern its underlying principles. They grapple with the profound questions that humanity has pondered for centuries, extending our knowledge and perspective to unfathomable distances. The challenges they encounter are met with resilience and creativity, while the rewards encompass the joy of discovery and the privilege of understanding the universe in all its splendor. As ambassadors of the cosmos, astronomers continue to guide us on a remarkable journey of exploration and enlightenment.

Harmony in Nature's Web:
An Ecologist's Exploration of
Ecosystem Dynamics

Ecology, the study of the intricate relationships between living organisms and their environment, emerges as a pivotal science in the face of our changing world. Ecologists take on the role of interpreters of nature's language, piecing together the puzzle of interconnected life forms and their surroundings. This section explores into the world of an ecologist, shedding light on the significance of ecology, the diverse roles ecologists play, the scientific methodologies they employ, the challenges they encounter, and the profound rewards they reap from understanding and conserving Earth's delicate ecosystems.

Ecology holds the key to understanding the intricate web of life on our planet. By studying the interactions between organisms and their environment, ecologists provide critical insights into the functioning and sustainability of ecosystems. This knowledge is vital for addressing pressing issues such as habitat loss, climate change, and species extinction. Ecologists serve as stewards of nature, guiding conservation efforts and advocating for the responsible use of resources to maintain a harmonious balance between human activities and the natural world.

Ecologists wear many hats, adapting their skills to various niches within the field. Conservation ecologists work to protect and restore endangered species and habitats. Behavioral ecologists delve into the intricacies of animal behavior and communication. Landscape ecologists study the spatial distribution of ecosystems and their connectivity. Urban ecologists explore the dynamics of nature in urban environments, and aquatic ecologists investigate the complex ecosystems of rivers, lakes, and oceans. Collectively, ecologists contribute to our holistic understanding of nature's interwoven tapestry.

The journey of an ecologist begins with close observation of natural environments. Whether in the wilderness or in the heart of the city, they collect data on species, populations, and environmental conditions. Ecologists employ various methodologies such as field surveys, experiments, statistical analyses, and computer modeling to make sense of the intricate relationships they uncover. They explore topics ranging from predator-prey dynamics to the impact of pollution on aquatic ecosystems. Collaboration with experts from other disciplines enriches their insights, contributing to a comprehensive understanding of ecological phenomena.

Being an ecologist comes with its own set of challenges. Fieldwork can be physically demanding, requiring ecologists to navigate remote and challenging terrains. The delicate balance between ecological research and human activities necessitates a nuanced approach to ethical considerations. Moreover, conveying the urgency of conservation efforts and influencing policy changes can be a daunting task. Yet, the rewards of being an ecologist are deeply gratifying. The joy of discovering hidden patterns in nature, the satisfaction of contributing to the preservation of ecosystems, and the ability to inspire others to appreciate and protect the environment are among the many rewards.

In conclusion, being an ecologist is a voyage of discovery and responsibility that uncovers the mysteries of life on Earth. Ecologists act as interpreters of nature's complex symphony, revealing the interdependence of species and their habitats. Through their dedication, they shape policies, guide conservation efforts, and foster an understanding of the vital connection between human well-being and the health of ecosystems. The challenges they face are met with a sense of purpose and urgency, while the rewards encompass the profound satisfaction of contributing to the welfare of our planet. As guardians of Earth's delicate balance, ecologists stand at the forefront of preserving the beauty and diversity of our natural world for generations to come.

Guiding Skies: The Precision and Responsibility of an Air Traffic Controller

In the bustling realm of aviation, air traffic controllers are the silent orchestrators who ensure the safety and efficiency of our skies. With split-second decisions and precise coordination, they guide aircraft through the complex and often congested airspace. This section adventures into the world of an air traffic controller, shedding light on the significance of their role, the diverse responsibilities they undertake, the specialized skills they wield, the challenges they face, and the profound impact they have on aviation safety.

Air traffic controllers are the unsung heroes of aviation, playing a pivotal role in maintaining the order and safety of our skies. They ensure that airplanes take off, land, and navigate in a seamless and organized manner, preventing collisions and mitigating risks. By managing aircraft movements and directing them around weather systems and congested airspace, air traffic controllers contribute to the efficient and reliable operation of the global aviation network.

Air traffic controllers shoulder a multitude of responsibilities that span both the ground and the air. They communicate with pilots to provide clear instructions, monitor radar displays to track aircraft positions, and coordinate takeoffs and landings at airports. En-route controllers manage aircraft as they cruise at high altitudes, ensuring safe separation and optimal routing. Approach and departure controllers guide planes during the critical phases of landing and takeoff, while tower controllers oversee aircraft movements on the runways and taxiways.

The role of an air traffic controller demands a unique skill set that blends precision, adaptability, and exceptional communication. Controllers must think quickly and remain composed in high-pressure situations, making split-second decisions to avert potential disasters. They undergo rigorous training programs that encompass theoretical knowledge, simulations, and on-the-job training in live environments. Controllers learn to manage stress, adapt to dynamic situations, and communicate effectively with pilots whose first language may not be English.

Being an air traffic controller comes with inherent challenges. The workload can be intense during peak travel times, and controllers must manage multiple aircraft simultaneously, often in adverse weather conditions. Miscommunications or errors can have severe consequences, highlighting the immense responsibility that controllers bear. Moreover, irregular working hours, including night shifts and weekends, can impact personal life. However, the rewards of the profession are significant. The sense of accomplishment in ensuring the safety of countless passengers, the excitement of orchestrating complex operations, and the opportunity to contribute to a critical aspect of modern society make the challenges worthwhile.

In conclusion, the role of an air traffic controller is both demanding and essential to the functioning of modern aviation. These skilled professionals work tirelessly behind the scenes, ensuring the safety and efficiency of the skies. The critical decisions they make, often in high-stress situations, impact the lives of countless individuals on a daily basis. The world of an air traffic controller is marked by precision, communication, and adaptability. Despite the challenges, the fulfillment derived from upholding aviation safety, the opportunity to engage with cutting-edge technology, and the satisfaction of contributing to the smooth operation of global air travel make being an air traffic controller an unparalleled and impactful career choice.

Beyond the Clouds: Life as a
Skies' Flight Attendant

Flight attendants, the faces of air travel, undertake a journey that goes beyond the clouds, offering passengers not just service but a sense of comfort and safety. With their impeccable hospitality, safety training, and ability to handle diverse situations, flight attendants play an essential role in making air travel a seamless and enjoyable experience. This section delves into the realm of a flight attendant, exploring the significance of their role, the dynamic responsibilities they manage, the skills they cultivate, the challenges they navigate, and the profound sense of adventure that accompanies those who take to the skies.

Flight attendants are more than just service providers; they are ambassadors of air travel, ensuring passengers' well-being and comfort while up in the air. They are responsible for maintaining a safe and secure environment onboard, while also delivering top-notch customer service. Flight attendants bridge the gap between passengers and the airline, embodying professionalism, empathy, and adaptability. They are integral to creating positive travel experiences, building passengers' trust and contributing to the airline's reputation.

The responsibilities of a flight attendant are multi-faceted and extend far beyond offering refreshments. They are trained to handle safety protocols, deliver pre-flight briefings, and respond effectively to emergencies. Ensuring passengers are secure during turbulence, assisting with boarding and disembarking, and managing various in-flight services are all part of their role. Flight attendants also play a crucial role in enforcing aviation regulations, maintaining order among passengers, and liaising with the flight crew for a seamless operation.

Being a successful flight attendant requires a versatile

skill set that includes excellent communication, problem-solving, and customer service skills. Clear communication is essential for delivering instructions, providing information, and calming anxious passengers. Flight attendants must have a keen eye for detail to detect any irregularities or safety concerns. Customer service excellence involves patience, empathy, and the ability to address various passenger needs, including those with special requirements. Additionally, the ability to remain composed under pressure and adapt to unpredictable situations is paramount for handling emergencies.

The life of a flight attendant comes with its own set of challenges. Irregular working hours, long flights, and time zone changes can disrupt normal routines and impact personal life. The potential for dealing with difficult passengers and managing unexpected emergencies can be mentally and emotionally demanding. However, the rewards are significant. The opportunity to travel to different destinations, experience diverse cultures, and form connections with fellow crew members are aspects that many find enriching. Moreover, the sense of accomplishment from ensuring passengers' safety, contributing to a smooth flight, and turning travel into a memorable experience make being a flight attendant uniquely fulfilling.

In conclusion, being a flight attendant is a dynamic and fulfilling journey that combines safety, hospitality, and adventure in the skies. Flight attendants are the unsung heroes who ensure that air travel is not just a means of transportation, but an experience that passengers remember fondly. Their significance extends beyond serving meals and beverages; they are responsible for creating a secure environment, addressing passenger needs, and providing comfort during the journey. Despite the challenges, the rewards of exploring new places, connecting with diverse passengers, and being part of a team that orchestrates seamless flights make being a flight attendant a remarkable career choice. Flight attendants stand as ambassadors of hospitality, demonstrating grace under pressure and making every flight a step towards new horizons.

Rails and Journeys: Life as a Train Conductor

In the realm of transportation, train conductors serve as the guardians of safety, order, and efficiency on the rails. With a firm grasp of protocols and a deep connection to the railways, they ensure the smooth operation of trains and the well-being of passengers. This section dives into the world of a train conductor, exploring the significance of their role, the diverse responsibilities they undertake, the skills they wield, the challenges they face, and the sense of purpose that comes from guiding trains and passengers to their destinations.

Train conductors hold a vital position in the world of rail travel, embodying the link between passengers, crew, and railway operations. They play a pivotal role in ensuring the safety and comfort of everyone on board, while also facilitating the punctuality and coordination of train schedules. Beyond their technical duties, conductors often become the face of the railway company, fostering positive experiences for passengers and contributing to the overall reputation of rail travel as a reliable and convenient mode of transportation.

The role of a train conductor encompasses a diverse array of responsibilities. Conductors oversee the boarding and disembarking of passengers, ensuring that tickets are checked and fares are collected. They manage onboard announcements, coordinate with other train crew members, and enforce safety regulations. In addition, conductors respond to emergencies and address passenger inquiries, providing a sense of security and assistance throughout the journey. Their watchful eyes on the train's interior and exterior contribute to the overall operation and maintenance of the railway system.

Being a train conductor demands a blend of technical expertise, communication skills, and situational awareness. Conductors must be adept at reading and interpreting schedules, understanding railway procedures, and utilizing communication devices. They interact with a diverse range of passengers, requiring effective interpersonal skills and a customer-oriented attitude. Moreover, their ability to adapt to unexpected situations and maintain a calm demeanor is crucial in the event of delays, disruptions, or emergencies.

The life of a train conductor is not without its challenges. Irregular working hours, including weekends and holidays, can disrupt personal routines. Conductors often work in varying weather conditions, from sweltering heat to freezing cold, while maintaining their professionalism and focus. Managing difficult passengers or handling stressful situations can also be demanding. Yet, the rewards are significant. The sense of responsibility in ensuring the safety of passengers and the smooth operation of trains, the opportunity to witness picturesque landscapes along the journey, and the satisfaction of contributing to an age-old mode of transportation imbue the role with deep meaning and fulfillment.

In conclusion, being a train conductor is a multifaceted role that intertwines operational excellence, customer service, and a commitment to safety. Conductors serve as the connective thread between passengers and the railway, embodying the spirit of travel and exploration. Their ability to navigate challenges, foster positive experiences, and uphold the standards of rail travel makes them invaluable contributors to the transportation industry. The role of a train conductor is marked by responsibility, adaptability, and a genuine connection to the rails and the passengers they serve.

On the Road: The Journey
of a Truck Driver

Truck drivers, the unsung heroes of the road, form an integral part of the modern economy by transporting goods across vast distances. With a constant view of ever-changing landscapes, truck drivers lead a unique and demanding lifestyle that is a blend of freedom and responsibility. This section explores into the world of a truck driver, exploring the significance of their role, the diverse experiences they encounter, the skills they master, the challenges they face, and the sense of purpose that propels them forward on the open road.

Truck drivers serve as the lifeline of the global supply chain, ensuring that goods reach their destinations promptly and safely. From food and clothing to electronics and machinery, the items we rely on daily often make their way to us thanks to the dedicated efforts of truck drivers. The movement of goods by road is the backbone of commerce, underscoring the indispensable role truck drivers play in sustaining economies and connecting communities.

The life of a truck driver is marked by a dynamic blend of experiences. They traverse diverse terrains, from urban centers to rural backroads, experiencing changing weather conditions and breathtaking landscapes along the way. The solitude of the road can be both liberating and isolating, allowing drivers to reflect and appreciate the beauty of the journey. Simultaneously, the camaraderie with fellow drivers and interactions with people at rest stops and delivery points bring a sense of community to an otherwise solitary profession.

Driving a large commercial vehicle demands a unique skill set that goes beyond navigating the roads. Truck drivers must possess a deep understanding of traffic rules, regulations, and safety protocols. They master the intricacies of maneuvering a heavy vehicle through tight spaces, backing into loading docks, and securing cargo properly. Time management and route planning become second nature, ensuring that deliveries are made efficiently while adhering to strict schedules.

The life of a truck driver is not without its challenges. Extended periods away from home and loved ones can strain personal relationships. Irregular schedules, including overnight shifts and long stretches on the road, can disrupt normal routines. The isolation and monotony of driving for extended hours can also take a toll on mental and physical well-being. However, the rewards are significant. The freedom of the open road, the opportunity to explore new places, and the satisfaction of being an essential part of the economy are among the many perks. Moreover, the sense of accomplishment that comes with successfully completing challenging routes and delivering goods on time is deeply gratifying.

In conclusion, being a truck driver is a journey that offers a unique blend of challenges, adventures, and responsibilities. These professionals embody the spirit of resilience, adaptability, and dedication as they navigate the highways and byways of the world. Their role goes beyond driving; it encompasses managing complex logistics, ensuring the safe transport of goods, and connecting communities. The significance of truck drivers extends far beyond the horizon they traverse, touching the lives of individuals and businesses in ways that often go unnoticed. Despite the hardships, the rewards of experiencing the open road, contributing to the economy, and forming connections with fellow drivers make being a truck driver a distinctive and purposeful career choice.

Steering Communities: The Role and Impact of a Bus Driver

Bus drivers, the steadfast navigators of urban and suburban landscapes, hold a crucial position in modern transportation systems. With their hands on the wheel and their eyes on the road, they ensure the smooth movement of people from one point to another. This section adventures into the world of a bus driver, exploring the significance of their role, the diverse responsibilities they shoulder, the skills they employ, the challenges they face, and the sense of fulfillment that comes from serving their communities through the daily commute.

Bus drivers serve as the backbone of public transportation systems, bridging the gap between various parts of a city or region. Their role is not merely about driving; it's about connecting communities, facilitating accessibility, and reducing traffic congestion. Bus drivers enable individuals from all walks of life to access education, employment, healthcare, and social activities. Their contributions extend beyond transportation; they are enablers of societal inclusivity and economic progress.

The responsibilities of a bus driver are multifaceted and extend beyond the act of driving. They manage passenger safety by ensuring that all individuals on board follow safety regulations and use seat belts when required. Bus drivers maintain schedules and routes, ensuring that passengers can rely on timely and efficient transportation. They offer assistance to individuals with special needs, answer passenger inquiries, and maintain order among a diverse group of passengers. Additionally, they are responsible for conducting routine checks and maintenance of their vehicles, ensuring that they are in optimal condition for safe travel.

Being a bus driver requires a unique blend of skills. They must possess a strong sense of responsibility and an acute awareness of their surroundings to ensure passenger safety. Patience, empathy, and effective communication are essential when dealing with various passenger personalities. Maneuvering a large vehicle through traffic, navigating congested streets, and dealing with unexpected road conditions demand quick thinking and adaptability. Moreover, maintaining a calm demeanor in the face of challenging situations is crucial for creating a positive travel experience for passengers.

The life of a bus driver is not without its challenges. Dealing with traffic congestion, adverse weather conditions, and navigating crowded streets can be stressful. Long hours, including split shifts and working weekends, can impact personal life and routines. The responsibility of ensuring passenger safety and managing diverse interactions requires a high level of attentiveness and professionalism. However, the rewards are substantial. The satisfaction of providing an essential service to the community, witnessing the positive impact of public transportation on people's lives, and forming connections with regular passengers are deeply gratifying aspects of the profession.

In conclusion, being a bus driver is a role that extends beyond the wheel and the road. Bus drivers are the threads that weave communities together, enabling mobility and fostering inclusivity. Their dedication to punctuality, safety, and passenger well-being is essential for the smooth functioning of urban and suburban life. Despite the challenges, the rewards of serving as a cornerstone of public transportation, contributing to a sustainable environment, and playing a role in the daily lives of countless individuals make being a bus driver a meaningful and impactful career choice. Bus drivers are the unsung heroes who keep our communities moving forward, one route at a time.

Guiding Champions: The Role of a Sports Coach in Athlete Development

Sports coaches, the architects of athletic success, stand as pivotal figures in the world of sports. With a blend of strategy, motivation, and mentorship, they guide athletes on a journey of growth, discipline, and triumph. This section delves into the realm of a sports coach, exploring the significance of their role, the multifaceted responsibilities they undertake, the skills they employ, the challenges they face, and the profound rewards they glean from shaping athletes into champions.

Sports coaches hold a pivotal role in fostering talent, refining skills, and nurturing a winning mindset. Beyond the realm of technique, they instill values such as discipline, teamwork, and perseverance that extend beyond the playing field. Coaches create an environment where athletes can thrive, pushing boundaries and reaching their full potential. Their influence transcends mere physical training, impacting athletes' personal development and shaping their character.

The responsibilities of a sports coach encompass a wide spectrum of roles. They design training programs tailored to the specific needs of individual athletes or teams, optimizing physical conditioning and skill development. Coaches provide technical guidance, analyzing performances and refining techniques. Moreover, they offer mentorship, building relationships based on trust and respect. Coaches act as motivators, instilling confidence and mental resilience in athletes to overcome challenges and setbacks.

Coaching demands a versatile skill set that goes beyond knowledge of the sport. Effective communication is paramount, as coaches must convey complex concepts in ways that resonate with athletes. Leadership skills are essential for guiding a team, managing conflicts, and fostering a positive team culture. Adaptability is crucial, as coaches must tailor strategies to various opponents and adapt to evolving circumstances. Additionally, emotional intelligence allows coaches to connect with athletes on a personal level, understanding their motivations, fears, and aspirations.

The life of a sports coach is not without its challenges. Balancing the technical and psychological aspects of coaching requires an intuitive understanding of human behavior. Coaches must navigate the pressures of competition, the weight of expectations, and the potential for criticism. Moreover, the emotional investment in athletes' successes and failures can be intense. However, the rewards are immeasurable. Witnessing athletes' growth, celebrating their triumphs, and knowing that one played a role in their journey is deeply gratifying. Coaches have the privilege of shaping athletes into confident, disciplined individuals who carry the lessons learned in sports into various facets of life.

In conclusion, being a sports coach is a dynamic endeavor that blends strategic acumen, leadership, and mentorship to nurture athletic excellence. Coaches hold a unique position as architects of athletes' growth, not only in the realm of sports but also in character development. Their contributions extend beyond wins and losses, shaping individuals who embody values of dedication, teamwork, and resilience. Despite the challenges, the rewards of witnessing athletes achieve their goals, the satisfaction of leaving a lasting impact, and the privilege of guiding individuals toward their best selves make being a sports coach a profoundly fulfilling journey. Coaches stand as pillars of inspiration, fostering greatness in others and leaving an indelible mark on the world of sports and beyond.

Epidemiology: Decoding Disease
Patterns for Public Health

Epidemiologists, the detectives of public health, work behind the scenes to understand and control the spread of diseases that impact communities. Armed with data analysis, research skills, and a commitment to public welfare, they contribute to the prevention and management of health crises. This section explores the realm of an epidemiologist, highlighting the significance of their role, the multifaceted responsibilities they undertake, the skills they refine, the challenges they tackle, and the satisfaction they derive from safeguarding public health through data-driven insights.

Epidemiologists play a vital role in shaping public health policies and strategies. By studying the distribution and determinants of diseases, they provide essential insights that inform preventive measures, interventions, and healthcare planning. Epidemiological research identifies risk factors, assesses disease trends, and helps in outbreak investigations. The work of epidemiologists extends to global health challenges, influencing decision-making at local, national, and international levels.

The responsibilities of an epidemiologist encompass a diverse range of tasks, from data collection and analysis to disease surveillance and intervention planning. They design and conduct studies to explore patterns of disease occurrence, contributing to our understanding of disease causation and progression. Epidemiologists also respond to disease outbreaks, tracing contacts and recommending control measures. Additionally, they collaborate with healthcare professionals, statisticians, policymakers, and communities to translate research findings into actionable public health strategies.

Being a successful epidemiologist demands a blend of scientific knowledge, analytical skills, and a commitment to the greater good. Epidemiologists must have a solid understanding of statistical methods and research design to accurately analyze and interpret data. Proficiency in data collection techniques, survey design, and modeling enhances their ability to draw meaningful conclusions. Effective communication skills are crucial for conveying findings to diverse audiences, from medical professionals to policymakers, and for building community trust during health crises.

The life of an epidemiologist comes with its own set of challenges. Disease outbreaks can be emotionally taxing, requiring quick responses and strategic decision-making. The unpredictability of infectious diseases demands adaptability and resilience. Additionally, dealing with complex datasets and statistical analyses can be intellectually demanding. However, the rewards are profound. The opportunity to contribute to the health and well-being of communities, prevent diseases, and save lives offers a strong sense of purpose. The impact of epidemiological findings on public health policies, the satisfaction of disease control, and the potential to address global health disparities make being an epidemiologist an exceptionally fulfilling career.

In conclusion, being an epidemiologist is a journey that merges scientific inquiry with a commitment to public health. Epidemiologists are the pillars of disease control, harnessing data and research to prevent and mitigate health crises. Their influence extends beyond research; they shape healthcare policies, interventions, and strategies that safeguard communities. Despite the challenges, the rewards of preventing outbreaks, improving health outcomes, and influencing healthcare on a societal scale create a profound sense of fulfillment. Epidemiologists stand as advocates for public health, embodying the quest for knowledge, the dedication to community well-being, and the pursuit of a healthier world for all.

Beyond the Surface: The Life and Science of a Dermatologist

Dermatologists, the custodians of skin health, embark on a journey that goes beyond mere aesthetics to explore the complexities of the body's largest organ. With their medical expertise, diagnostic acumen, and compassionate care, they address a wide array of skin conditions, from common concerns to life-threatening diseases. This section dives into the world of a dermatologist, exploring the significance of their role, the multifaceted responsibilities they shoulder, the skills they refine, the challenges they overcome, and the profound satisfaction they derive from promoting skin wellness and enhancing the lives of their patients.

Dermatologists hold a pivotal role in healthcare, as skin health impacts both physical and mental well-being. Beyond addressing cosmetic concerns, dermatologists diagnose and treat a diverse range of skin conditions, from acne and eczema to skin cancer. Skin conditions can often be reflective of underlying health issues, making dermatologists vital in diagnosing systemic diseases. Their work also extends to improving patients' self-esteem and confidence, emphasizing the interconnectedness of physical and mental health.

The responsibilities of a dermatologist encompass a broad spectrum of tasks, including diagnosing and treating skin conditions, performing dermatological surgeries, and educating patients about skin health. They evaluate skin concerns, prescribe medications, and recommend skincare regimens tailored to individual needs. Dermatologists also conduct surgical procedures, such as mole removals or skin biopsies. Furthermore, they offer guidance on sun protection, skin cancer prevention, and lifestyle choices that impact skin health.

Being a successful dermatologist requires a blend of medical knowledge, clinical skill, and patient-centered care.

Dermatologists must possess a deep understanding of skin anatomy, physiology, and pathology to accurately diagnose and treat conditions. Proficiency in dermatological procedures, such as chemical peels, laser treatments, and minor surgical interventions, is essential. Effective communication skills are vital for establishing rapport with patients, explaining diagnoses and treatment options, and addressing their concerns and anxieties.

The life of a dermatologist comes with its own set of challenges. Diagnosing skin conditions can be intricate, requiring attention to detail and thorough examination. Balancing patient loads, especially when dealing with chronic conditions or skin emergencies, can be demanding. The ever-evolving landscape of dermatological advancements also demands continuous learning and adaptation. However, the rewards are profound. The satisfaction of relieving patients' discomfort, treating chronic conditions, and diagnosing potentially life-threatening diseases is immeasurable. Moreover, witnessing the transformation of patients' confidence and well-being as their skin health improves is deeply gratifying.

In conclusion, being a dermatologist is a dynamic journey that blends medical expertise with empathetic care. Dermatologists serve as guardians of skin health, promoting wellness, diagnosing conditions, and improving patients' quality of life. Their influence extends beyond treating skin concerns; they impact overall health and self-esteem. Despite the challenges, the rewards of healing skin conditions, enhancing confidence, and diagnosing critical diseases create a sense of fulfillment unique to the profession. Dermatologists stand as advocates for skin health, embodying the pursuit of wellness, self-assurance, and the profound impact of healthy skin on holistic well-being.

Aligning Health: The Journey of a Chiropractor

Chiropractors, the practitioners of spinal alignment and holistic health, play a distinctive role in promoting well-being by focusing on the body's natural healing abilities. With their specialized knowledge, hands-on techniques, and patient-centered approach, they aim to alleviate pain, enhance mobility, and improve overall quality of life. This section explores into the world of a chiropractor, exploring the significance of their role, the comprehensive responsibilities they undertake, the skills they hone, the challenges they navigate, and the fulfillment they experience in empowering individuals to achieve optimal health through balanced alignment.

Chiropractors hold a unique position in healthcare, emphasizing the importance of spinal health and its impact on the nervous system. By addressing misalignments in the spine, chiropractors seek to enhance the body's innate ability to heal and function optimally. Their work spans beyond treating pain; it contributes to promoting the body's self-regulation, stress reduction, and overall well-being. Chiropractors are essential in both preventive care and as partners in addressing chronic pain and musculoskeletal conditions.

The responsibilities of a chiropractor encompass a wide array of tasks, from conducting patient assessments and diagnosing conditions to delivering hands-on adjustments and providing lifestyle guidance. Chiropractors carefully evaluate patients' medical history, perform physical examinations, and often utilize diagnostic imaging to understand the root causes of discomfort. They employ a variety of techniques, such as spinal adjustments, joint mobilization, and soft tissue therapies, to correct misalignments and enhance bodily function. Additionally, chiropractors educate patients about ergonomics, exercise, and nutrition to support their long-term well-being.

Being a successful chiropractor requires a blend of anatomical knowledge, manual dexterity, and effective communication skills. Chiropractors must possess a deep understanding of human anatomy, particularly the musculoskeletal and nervous systems, to identify and address spinal misalignments. Proficiency in various adjustment techniques, including spinal manipulation and mobilization, is essential for safe and effective patient care. Moreover, strong interpersonal skills are crucial for building trust, understanding patients' needs, and guiding them through their journey to improved health.

The life of a chiropractor comes with its own set of challenges. Diagnosing conditions accurately requires attention to detail and the ability to differentiate between various sources of pain. Balancing patient loads and addressing diverse needs, from acute injuries to chronic conditions, can be demanding. Moreover, chiropractors need to stay informed about the latest advancements in their field. However, the rewards are profound. The satisfaction of witnessing patients experience pain relief, regain mobility, and improve their overall quality of life is deeply gratifying. The opportunity to make a positive impact on individuals' health and well-being, without solely relying on pharmaceutical interventions, is a rewarding aspect of the profession.

In conclusion, being a chiropractor is a dynamic journey that centers around restoring balance, mobility, and well-being. Chiropractors serve as advocates for natural healing, empowering individuals to achieve health and vitality through spinal alignment and holistic approaches. Their influence extends beyond relieving pain; they contribute to overall wellness, vitality, and a higher quality of life. Despite the challenges, the rewards of facilitating positive transformations, restoring alignment, and empowering individuals to take charge of their health create a profound sense of purpose. Chiropractors stand as advocates for holistic health, embodying the principles of balance, harmony, and the innate potential of the human body to thrive.

Harmonizing Senses: The Odyssey
of an Otolaryngologist

Otolaryngologists, the experts of the head and neck, navigate the intricacies of the senses—sight, sound, and smell. With their profound medical knowledge, precision techniques, and commitment to patient well-being, they diagnose and treat conditions ranging from hearing loss to sinus disorders. This section adventures into the world of an otolaryngologist, exploring the significance of their role, the multifaceted responsibilities they shoulder, the skills they master, the challenges they conquer, and the satisfaction they derive from restoring and enhancing sensory experiences.

Otolaryngologists are integral to maintaining the delicate balance of our sensory systems. They diagnose and treat conditions that impact hearing, balance, voice, and the upper respiratory tract. Otolaryngologists are pivotal in addressing not only medical concerns but also conditions that affect communication, appearance, and quality of life. By specializing in the complex anatomy of the head and neck, they contribute to the overall well-being and functionality of their patients.

The responsibilities of an otolaryngologist encompass a broad spectrum of tasks, from diagnosing conditions and performing surgeries to providing preventive care and patient education. Otolaryngologists evaluate patients with symptoms such as hearing loss, sinus issues, voice disorders, and more. They employ specialized tools and techniques, such as endoscopes, imaging, and auditory tests, to accurately diagnose conditions. Otolaryngologists also perform surgical interventions to address issues like tonsillectomies, rhinoplasties, and cochlear implants, while also offering guidance on preventive measures and lifestyle adjustments.

Being a successful otolaryngologist demands a blend of medical acumen, surgical skill, and empathetic patient care. Otolaryngologists must possess in-depth knowledge of the anatomy and physiology of the head and neck to accurately diagnose and treat conditions. Proficiency in surgical techniques, ranging from delicate microsurgeries to complex reconstructive procedures, is essential. Effective communication skills are crucial for building rapport with patients, explaining diagnoses and treatment options, and providing emotional support during times of vulnerability.

The life of an otolaryngologist presents its own set of challenges. Diagnosing and treating conditions involving intricate structures demands precision and a deep understanding of potential complications. Balancing the demands of patient care, surgical procedures, and administrative tasks can be demanding. Moreover, the fast-paced nature of medical advancements requires continuous learning to stay up-to-date. However, the rewards are profound. The satisfaction of restoring hearing, alleviating discomfort, and improving patients' quality of life is immeasurable. Witnessing patients regain their ability to communicate, breathe freely, and experience the world around them brings a deep sense of fulfillment.

In conclusion, being an otolaryngologist is a journey that intertwines medical expertise with compassionate care. Otolaryngologists are the orchestrators of sensory harmony, diagnosing and treating conditions that impact sight, sound, and smell. Their influence extends beyond medical procedures; they restore communication, enhance well-being, and empower patients to regain their sensory experiences. Despite the challenges, the rewards of transformative interventions, restored quality of life, and improved communication make being an otolaryngologist a uniquely fulfilling career. Otolaryngologists stand as champions of sensory health, embodying the pursuit of equilibrium, restoration, and the empowerment of the senses.

Navigating the Realm of Sedation:
The Journey of an Anesthesiologist

Anesthesiologists, the orchestrators of controlled unconsciousness, play a critical role in the realm of medical care by ensuring patients' comfort and safety during surgeries and procedures. With their expertise in administering anesthesia and monitoring vital signs, they stand as guardians of patients' well-being in the delicate interlude between consciousness and unconsciousness. This section delves into the world of an anesthesiologist, exploring the significance of their role, the multifaceted responsibilities they shoulder, the skills they refine, the challenges they confront, and the fulfillment they derive from their pivotal contributions to the surgical process.

Anesthesiologists are integral to modern healthcare, as they enable patients to undergo surgeries and procedures without experiencing pain or distress. Beyond pain management, they ensure physiological stability during the critical period of medical interventions. Anesthesiologists possess a profound understanding of the body's responses to anesthesia and medications, allowing them to tailor their approach to each patient's unique needs. Their work is not only about administering drugs; it's about orchestrating a symphony of physiological adjustments that ensure patient safety and comfort.

The responsibilities of an anesthesiologist encompass a wide spectrum of tasks, from preoperative patient assessment and anesthesia administration to postoperative monitoring and pain management. Anesthesiologists evaluate patients' medical history and conduct thorough physical examinations to determine the appropriate anesthesia plan. During procedures, they monitor patients' vital signs, administer anesthesia drugs, and adjust doses as needed to maintain anesthesia depth and stability. Post-operatively, anesthesiologists manage pain and ensure a smooth transition to consciousness.

Being a successful anesthesiologist demands a blend of medical knowledge, technical skills, and adaptability. Anesthesiologists must possess an in-depth understanding of pharmacology, physiology, and the interactions between drugs and the body. Proficiency in various anesthesia techniques, such as general anesthesia, regional anesthesia, and sedation, is essential. Effective communication skills are crucial for building trust with patients, explaining anesthesia options, and collaborating with surgical teams.

The life of an anesthesiologist presents its own set of challenges. Each patient's response to anesthesia can vary, demanding quick thinking and adjustments to ensure patient safety. The high-stress environment of the operating room requires composure and teamwork. Additionally, anesthesiologists need to stay current with advancements in anesthesia drugs, equipment, and monitoring techniques. However, the rewards are profound. The satisfaction of ensuring patients' comfort, enabling successful surgeries, and playing a vital role in healthcare teams' success is immeasurable. Witnessing patients emerge from anesthesia with relief and gratitude underscores the meaningful impact of the profession.

In conclusion, being an anesthesiologist is a journey of scientific precision, adaptability, and patient-centered care. Anesthesiologists are the architects of controlled unconsciousness, ensuring patients' safety and well-being throughout medical procedures. Their influence extends beyond the surgical theater; they enable medical interventions, alleviate pain, and create a bridge between consciousness and recovery. Despite the challenges, the rewards of contributing to successful surgeries, witnessing patients' relief, and knowing that their expertise makes a significant difference in patient outcomes make being an anesthesiologist a profoundly fulfilling career. Anesthesiologists stand as sentinels of comfort and safety, embodying the commitment to patients' well-being and the art of orchestrating the delicate balance between consciousness and the void.

Illuminating the Invisible: The Exploration of a Radiologist

Radiologists, the interpreters of hidden stories within the human body, navigate the intricate landscapes of medical imaging to provide insights that shape diagnoses and treatment plans. With their expertise in deciphering images produced by various modalities, they play a pivotal role in modern medicine. This section dives into the world of a radiologist, exploring the significance of their role, the multifaceted responsibilities they shoulder, the skills they master, the challenges they embrace, and the satisfaction they derive from being the bridge between technology and patient care.

Radiologists stand as essential figures in healthcare, enabling accurate diagnoses through the analysis of medical images. They collaborate with other medical professionals to unravel mysteries that are concealed within X-rays, MRIs, CT scans, and more. Radiologists contribute to the early detection of diseases, the assessment of treatment effectiveness, and the guidance for surgical interventions. Their work spans across various medical specialties, making them integral to healthcare teams.

The responsibilities of a radiologist encompass a wide spectrum of tasks, from reviewing medical images and interpreting findings to communicating results with other medical practitioners. Radiologists assess the quality and relevance of images, identify anomalies or abnormalities, and provide concise and detailed reports. They also play a crucial role in guiding other healthcare professionals in selecting appropriate imaging techniques and protocols for specific clinical scenarios.

Being a successful radiologist requires a blend of medical knowledge, analytical skills, and an eye for detail. Radiologists must have an in-depth understanding of human anatomy, pathology, and the principles behind various imaging modalities. Proficiency in image interpretation, pattern recognition, and data analysis is essential. Moreover, effective communication skills are crucial for conveying complex findings to colleagues who may not be as familiar with imaging techniques.

The life of a radiologist presents its own set of challenges. Deciphering intricate images requires a meticulous approach, as small details can hold significant diagnostic value. The continuous advancement of imaging technology demands ongoing learning to stay updated with new techniques and modalities. Radiologists also need to balance high patient volumes with maintaining quality interpretations. However, the rewards are profound. The satisfaction of contributing to accurate diagnoses, enabling timely interventions, and directly impacting patient outcomes creates a sense of accomplishment. Radiologists witness the tangible impact of their work as patients receive the right treatment at the right time.

In conclusion, being a radiologist is a journey of visual exploration, medical expertise, and diagnostic mastery. Radiologists are the detectives of the medical world, uncovering insights that guide medical decisions. Their influence extends beyond technology; they are the bridge between the world of images and the realm of patient care. Despite the challenges, the rewards of solving medical puzzles, enabling precise interventions, and making a difference in patients' lives underscore the essential nature of this profession. Radiologists stand as interpreters of the body's stories, embodying the commitment to accuracy, collaboration, and the pursuit of medical excellence.

Eradicating Pests: Life as an Exterminator

Exterminators, the unsung heroes of pest control, work tirelessly to rid our living spaces of unwanted intruders that threaten health and comfort. Armed with specialized knowledge, effective techniques, and a dedication to maintaining hygiene, they ensure that homes and businesses remain safe and pest-free. This section explores into the world of an exterminator, exploring the significance of their role, the diverse challenges they face, the skills they master, the rewards they reap, and the crucial service they provide in maintaining the quality of human habitation.

Exterminators play a vital role in safeguarding public health and preserving property. Pests can spread diseases, damage structures, and compromise the cleanliness of living spaces. Exterminators act as protectors, preventing infestations and controlling pest populations. Their work extends beyond eliminating nuisances; it ensures the safety, comfort, and well-being of individuals and communities.

The responsibilities of an exterminator encompass a wide range of tasks, from inspecting premises and identifying pests to implementing control strategies and educating clients. Exterminators start by identifying the type of pests and the extent of infestation. They design customized treatment plans, which may involve the use of pesticides, traps, and preventive measures. Exterminators also educate clients on pest prevention techniques, such as proper waste management and sealing entry points, to avoid future infestations.

Being a successful exterminator requires a blend of knowledge, skill, and attention to detail. Exterminators must have a deep understanding of pest biology, behavior, and environmental factors that contribute to infestations. Proficiency in the use of various pest control methods, including chemical, biological, and mechanical techniques, is essential. Effective communication skills are crucial for discussing treatment options with clients, explaining the safety precautions of pesticide use, and providing guidance on pest prevention.

The life of an exterminator comes with its own set of challenges. Working in various environments, from homes to commercial establishments, demands adaptability and flexibility. Dealing with toxic chemicals requires strict adherence to safety protocols. Additionally, exterminators need to stay updated with the latest pest control methods and regulations. However, the rewards are meaningful. The satisfaction of seeing the immediate impact of their work, restoring comfort to clients' lives, and contributing to public health creates a sense of accomplishment. Moreover, the ability to solve unique pest challenges fosters a continuous learning experience.

In conclusion, being an exterminator is a journey of vigilance, knowledge, and service. Exterminators fulfill a crucial role in maintaining hygienic living environments, safeguarding property, and preserving human health. Their influence extends beyond pest control; they contribute to the well-being and peace of mind of individuals and communities. Despite the challenges, the rewards of solving pest-related issues, improving living conditions, and protecting health and property underscore the essential nature of this profession. Exterminators stand as defenders against unseen invaders, embodying the commitment to cleanliness, safety, and the harmonious coexistence of humans and their environment.

Tracing Threads of Infrastructure: Adventures in Utility Locating

In the intricate tapestry of modern urban life, there exists a hidden world that most people rarely acknowledge —the vast network of underground utilities that power our cities. The individuals responsible for unveiling this invisible infrastructure are utility locators, unsung heroes who work tirelessly to ensure the smooth functioning of society. This section adventures into the fascinating and often challenging life of a utility locator, examining their crucial role, the skills they require, the technology they wield, the challenges they face, and the satisfaction derived from a job well done.

Utility locators serve as the guiding light through the labyrinth of pipes, cables, and conduits that lie beneath our feet. Their primary role is to identify and mark the location of underground utilities, preventing accidental damage during construction and excavation projects. Without their expertise, a simple dig could lead to catastrophic consequences, disrupting essential services like water, electricity, gas, and communication. Utility locators act as guardians of the hidden world, ensuring the safety of both workers and the community at large.

The job of a utility locator demands a unique blend of skills. Attention to detail, problem-solving ability, and a strong spatial sense are crucial. Locators must interpret maps and blueprints, use specialized equipment, and apply their knowledge of utility systems to pinpoint their exact locations. Technological advancements have revolutionized the field, with tools like ground-penetrating radar and electromagnetic sensors enabling locators to "see" beneath the ground. The ability to adapt to and master these cutting-edge technologies is essential for success in this profession.

While the job of a utility locator is rewarding, it

is not without its challenges. Working conditions can be harsh, ranging from extreme weather conditions to tight spaces and remote locations. Additionally, the accuracy of existing utility maps may vary, leading to uncertainties and surprises. The pressure to work quickly and efficiently while maintaining accuracy can be stressful. Moreover, locators often interact with construction crews and contractors, requiring strong communication skills to ensure that their findings are understood and respected.

Amidst the challenges, utility locators find profound satisfaction in their work. Their efforts contribute to the safe and smooth progress of construction projects, helping to prevent accidents, minimize disruptions, and save costs. Locators take pride in knowing that their work is essential for the functioning of a modern society and that they play a pivotal role in maintaining the unseen infrastructure that sustains it. This sense of purpose and the tangible impact of their work are powerful motivators that keep utility locators dedicated to their craft.

In the hustle and bustle of urban life, the world beneath our feet often goes unnoticed. However, the role of utility locators is a testament to the significance of what lies underground. Their skills, dedication, and the advanced technologies they wield ensure that our cities continue to thrive without disruptions. Despite the challenges they face, the satisfaction of safeguarding the invisible web of utilities and contributing to the smooth functioning of society make being a utility locator a truly noble and fulfilling profession. As we walk the streets above, it is essential to remember the individuals who make it all possible by navigating the depths beneath.

Charting the Uncharted: Navigating Terrain as a Surveyor

In the realm of mapping, land development, and construction, there exists an often-unseen force that shapes our physical environment with meticulous accuracy—the surveyor. This section delves into the captivating world of surveyors, shedding light on their vital role, the skills they command, the advanced technology they employ, the challenges they encounter, and the profound satisfaction derived from their work.

Surveyors are the architects of precise spatial information. They play an indispensable role in mapping and measuring land, creating accurate representations of the Earth's surface that serve as the foundation for construction, property boundaries, infrastructure development, and various other projects. Surveyors ensure that buildings rise level and true, that roads wind along accurate paths, and that cities expand without encroaching on one another. Their work forms the bedrock upon which countless human activities rest, quietly shaping the contours of the world we inhabit.

The job of a surveyor necessitates a blend of technical skills, mathematical prowess, and an astute eye for detail. Surveyors are proficient in using precision instruments such as total stations, GPS receivers, and laser scanners to measure distances, angles, and elevations with exceptional accuracy. Their proficiency in interpreting legal documents, maps, and blueprints is crucial for establishing property boundaries and resolving disputes. Moreover, their spatial thinking ability enables them to mentally visualize and understand the layout of complex landscapes.

Surveying has been dramatically transformed by technological advancements. Traditional chain measurements have given way to electronic distance measurements (EDM), and theodolites have evolved into robotic total stations capable of remote operation. Global Positioning System (GPS) technology enables surveyors to pinpoint locations with unprecedented precision, while LiDAR (Light Detection and Ranging) technology facilitates the creation of highly detailed 3D models of terrain. Geographic Information Systems (GIS) software empowers surveyors to manage, analyze, and visualize vast amounts of spatial data, streamlining their workflow and enhancing the accuracy of their results.

While surveying is a fulfilling profession, it comes with its own set of challenges. Surveyors often work outdoors in varying weather conditions, encountering physical obstacles and difficult terrain. Additionally, the complexity of landownership laws and property rights can lead to legal disputes, requiring surveyors to navigate intricate legal frameworks. The pressure to deliver precise results within tight deadlines can be demanding. Despite these challenges, the rewards are numerous. Surveyors take pride in their contribution to infrastructure development, environmental conservation, and disaster management. The joy of seeing a completed project rise in alignment with their measurements is a testament to the value of their expertise.

Surveying is a profession that bridges artistry and science, combining mathematical rigor with a deep appreciation for the physical world. Surveyors find fulfillment in the accuracy they bring to their work, knowing that their measurements serve as the groundwork for vital structures and systems. Whether mapping out a new road, establishing property boundaries, or assisting in environmental conservation, surveyors witness the tangible impact of their efforts. The satisfaction of meticulously charting the terrain, ensuring its accuracy, and contributing to the built environment is what keeps surveyors inspired and dedicated to their craft.

Surveyors are the silent architects of our urban

landscapes, mapping the world with meticulous precision and shaping the physical realm with their expertise. Their mastery of technology, mathematics, and spatial thinking allows them to translate the complexities of the Earth into coherent plans and measurements. While their work often goes unnoticed by the general public, the impact of surveyors reverberates throughout the infrastructure and development projects that define modern society. Their role is not just about measuring distances; it's about translating vision into reality, turning blueprints into thriving communities, and ensuring that the physical world conforms to the imaginative constructs of humankind. The work of a surveyor is an essential thread woven into the fabric of progress, silently connecting the dots that shape the world we live in.

Guardians of the Wilderness: Navigating Life as a Park Ranger

Amidst the bustling modern world, where technology and urbanization dominate, there exists a group of dedicated individuals who stand as custodians of the natural world – park rangers. These unsung heroes are entrusted with the crucial task of preserving and protecting our planet's most precious landscapes and wildlife. Being a park ranger transcends beyond a profession; it's a calling that demands passion, dedication, and a profound love for nature. This section dives into the multifaceted world of park rangers, exploring their roles as stewards, educators, law enforcers, and ambassadors of wilderness.

At the heart of a park ranger's duty lies the role of a steward – a guardian entrusted with safeguarding the natural beauty and ecological balance of protected areas. Park rangers serve as the frontline defense against environmental degradation, human impact, and encroachment on delicate ecosystems. Through meticulous monitoring, conservation efforts, and habitat restoration, they ensure that the pristine landscapes remain untouched by the ravages of time. Whether it's a towering forest, a rugged mountain range, or a serene coastline, park rangers work tirelessly to maintain the integrity of these spaces for present and future generations.

Beyond their conservation responsibilities, park rangers take on the mantle of educators and ambassadors of nature. Through guided tours, interpretive programs, and educational workshops, they foster a deeper connection between visitors and the natural world. By imparting knowledge about local flora, fauna, geology, and historical significance, rangers inspire a sense of wonder and appreciation. They play a pivotal role in nurturing environmental awareness and promoting responsible behavior among visitors. This educational aspect of their role creates a ripple effect, as visitors carry the lessons they learn from rangers into their own lives, thereby contributing to a more sustainable future.

While the beauty of nature beckons countless visitors, the human impact can sometimes be detrimental. Park rangers are responsible for enforcing regulations that protect the delicate balance of ecosystems and ensure the safety of visitors. Their role involves preventing activities that could harm wildlife, damage natural features, or disrupt the tranquility of the environment. With authority and diplomacy, rangers educate visitors about proper conduct and intervene when necessary to maintain order. This enforcement role is not just about upholding laws but also about instilling a sense of ethical responsibility towards the environment.

Park rangers serve as a vital link between the wilderness and the outside world. Their presence provides visitors with a connection to the untamed beauty that lies beyond urban landscapes. As knowledgeable guides, rangers help visitors navigate the trails, providing insights that enhance the outdoor experience. They often share stories of the land's history, indigenous cultures, and ecological significance, fostering a deeper appreciation for the places they protect. In remote and wild settings, rangers become sources of guidance and reassurance, ensuring that adventurers can explore with confidence and respect for nature's wonders.

Being a park ranger is more than a job; it's a way of life. The commitment required to live and work in remote, often challenging environments showcases the dedication rangers possess. The isolation, unpredictable weather, and physical demands are met with a spirit of resilience and a passion for the cause. Park rangers form a close-knit community bound by their shared values and devotion to the natural world. This personal calling drives them to face the trials and triumphs of the profession with unwavering determination.

Park rangers are the unsung heroes who safeguard the planet's last vestiges of untouched beauty. Their multifaceted role as stewards, educators, enforcers, and liaisons to nature encapsulates their dedication to preserving Earth's most cherished landscapes. The legacy they leave extends beyond the boundaries of the parks they protect – it's woven into the fabric of a global movement towards conservation and sustainability. In their tireless efforts, park rangers inspire us to rekindle our connection with the natural world, reminding us that the call of the wild is a call we must heed for the sake of our planet's future.

Guiding Journeys: Unveiling the
Art of Being a Tour Guide

In a world where travel is a cornerstone of exploration and self-discovery, tour guides emerge as the storytellers and companions of our journeys. Beyond their functional role of providing information, tour guides are the weavers of narratives, the conduits to culture, and the orchestrators of experiences. Being a tour guide entails more than reciting facts; it involves fostering connections, sharing insights, and creating memories that linger long after the journey concludes. This section explores into the dynamic world of tour guiding, exploring the art of storytelling, cultural diplomacy, adaptability, and the human touch that defines this profession.

At the heart of tour guiding lies the art of storytelling. Tour guides transform historical facts, architectural details, and local legends into narratives that breathe life into the places they lead visitors through. Through their words, they transport travelers across time, immersing them in the tales that have shaped destinations. Whether describing the intrigue of ancient ruins or the resilience of a local community, tour guides capture the essence of a place, bridging the gap between past and present. This skill is not merely about relaying information but about building an emotional connection between travelers and the locations they explore.

Tour guides play a unique role in cultural diplomacy, acting as cultural ambassadors who facilitate cross-cultural understanding. They possess the ability to bridge gaps of language, customs, and traditions, introducing visitors to the nuances of a foreign culture. By fostering respectful interactions, showcasing local customs, and encouraging immersive experiences, guides promote empathy and cultural exchange. In a world seeking to break down barriers, tour guides serve as conduits for promoting appreciation and respect for diversity.

The life of a tour guide is characterized by fluidity and adaptability. No two tours are the same, as groups vary in size, interests, and expectations. Guides must possess the agility to tailor their narratives to suit their audience while remaining authentic to the destination. From school groups eager to learn to adventurous travelers seeking hidden gems, guides must pivot their approach to cater to diverse demographics. This adaptability extends beyond content; guides also navigate unexpected challenges, from sudden weather changes to logistical hiccups. Their capacity to maintain composure and adapt on the go is a testament to their professionalism and resilience.

In the age of technology, where information is readily available at our fingertips, the value of human connection has never been more pronounced. Tour guides offer a personal touch that digital platforms cannot replicate. They forge connections with travelers, sharing their passion for a destination and engaging in genuine interactions. Through their insights and anecdotes, guides transform mundane facts into captivating narratives. These connections create an environment where questions are encouraged, stories are shared, and travelers gain a deeper appreciation for the places they explore.

The role of a tour guide extends beyond the duration of a tour; it resides in the memories they leave behind. A well-guided tour becomes a tapestry of experiences that travelers carry with them long after they return home. These memories are not limited to landmarks visited; they encompass the laughter shared, the friendships formed, and the intangible connections to a place. The impact of a skilled guide can shape travelers' perceptions, fostering a love for exploration and a desire to continue discovering the world. The legacy of a tour guide lives on through the stories retold, the photographs shared, and the inspiration sparked.

Tour guides are the architects of memories, the guardians of culture, and the storytellers of our journeys. Their profession embodies a delicate blend of information dissemination and emotional connection. Through the art of storytelling, cultural diplomacy, adaptability, and the magic of personal interactions, tour guides craft experiences that resonate deep within the hearts of travelers. They facilitate connections that transcend borders and foster a global community bound by shared stories and a love for exploration. In the landscapes they guide us through, tour guides create not just experiences but a profound sense of belonging to the world.

Keys to Clarity: Life as a Skilled Typist

In the digital age, where communication and information dissemination occur at the speed of keystrokes, the role of a typist remains essential. Typists are the skilled individuals who transform thoughts, ideas, and information into written form with accuracy and efficiency. Their work spans various industries, from administrative roles to creative endeavors, and their expertise contributes to effective communication and documentation. This section explores the nuanced world of typists, shedding light on the significance of their role, the evolution of typing skills, the challenges they face, their impact on productivity, and the vital link between their craft and modern communication.

Typists play a pivotal role in the seamless transfer of thoughts from the mind to the written page. Their skillset transcends mere transcription; they are the conduits through which spoken words and handwritten drafts transform into polished, well-structured documents. Typists enable effective communication, ensuring that ideas are presented clearly, professionally, and with a touch of finesse. Their work contributes to the authenticity and credibility of documents, whether they are business reports, creative works, academic papers, or legal documents. The precision of their keystrokes underpins the smooth functioning of modern communication.

The evolution of typing skills reflects the changing landscape of technology. While traditional typewriters once dominated the typing scene, the advent of computers and digital interfaces has revolutionized the field. Typists have transitioned from punching keys on mechanical devices to tapping keys on sleek keyboards, adapting their skills to various input methods. Modern typists often possess proficiency in touch typing, where they rely on muscle memory to type without looking at the keyboard. This evolution underscores the adaptability of typists, who seamlessly integrate their craft with technological advancements.

The digital era has introduced both opportunities and challenges for typists. While modern technology offers faster typing speeds and convenient editing tools, it also places a premium on multitasking and digital literacy. Typists must navigate an array of software applications, collaborate remotely, and manage electronic documents efficiently. Additionally, the pressure to produce content quickly can lead to errors if not managed carefully. The challenge lies not only in technical proficiency but also in maintaining focus and accuracy in an environment characterized by constant distractions.

Typists significantly impact productivity and professionalism in various sectors. Administrative typists ensure that office communications and documents are well-crafted, contributing to efficient workflows. Transcriptionists convert spoken content into written records, aiding in record keeping and data analysis. Creative writers and authors rely on typists to transform handwritten drafts into polished manuscripts. In academic and research settings, typists assist in producing accurate and well-structured papers. The contribution of typists extends to legal proceedings, medical documentation, and more. Their role elevates the quality and professionalism of written content, enabling professionals to focus on their core tasks.

The work of typists intersects with the broader landscape of modern communication. In an age where written communication is omnipresent – from emails and social media posts to official documents and books – the role of typists remains relevant. Their ability to transform ideas into well-organized text resonates with the essence of effective communication. As technology continues to evolve, the expertise of typists evolves as well, adapting to new tools and methods while preserving the essence of their craft.

Typists are the unsung heroes behind the written word, diligently weaving the fabric of communication that connects societies, industries, and individuals. Their keystrokes bridge the gap between ideas and tangible documents, ensuring accuracy, clarity, and professionalism. In a world of rapid technological change, typists demonstrate their adaptability and commitment to their craft, embracing new tools while preserving the art of precision typing. As long as the written word remains a cornerstone of human interaction, the role of typists will continue to be indispensable, reflecting the synergy between skill, technology, and effective communication.

A Heartwarming Journey: Chronicles of a Caregiver's Dedication

In the intricate web of human relationships, the role of a caregiver stands as a beacon of compassion, empathy, and selflessness. This section adventures into the world of caregivers, exploring their essential role, the qualities they embody, the challenges they confront, the rewards they reap, and the profound impact they have on both individuals and society as a whole.

Caregivers hold a unique and crucial position in society, providing assistance, support, and companionship to those in need. Whether caring for the elderly, individuals with disabilities, or those facing health challenges, caregivers become pillars of strength for those they serve. They assist with daily tasks, administer medications, offer emotional support, and create an environment of comfort and security. The essence of caregiving lies in the genuine desire to alleviate suffering, improve quality of life, and foster a sense of dignity and independence for those they care for.

Caregivers possess a profound blend of qualities that make them the heart and soul of their vocation. Empathy tops the list—a caregiver's ability to understand and share the feelings of another is the foundation of building a meaningful connection. Patience becomes a virtue as they navigate challenging situations and varying moods. Flexibility allows them to adapt to the evolving needs of those they care for, while resilience helps them cope with the emotional demands of their role. Above all, compassion is the driving force that fuels their commitment, ensuring that their care is not just a duty, but a genuine act of kindness.

The role of a caregiver is not without its challenges. Caregivers often grapple with physical and emotional exhaustion as they juggle their own lives with the demands of caregiving. Witnessing the struggles of their loved ones or patients can take an emotional toll, leading to burnout and compassion fatigue. Moreover, balancing personal boundaries while maintaining a close and caring relationship requires delicate navigation. Financial constraints, lack of support, and the intricate medical needs of those under their care add further layers of complexity. Yet, caregivers rise above these challenges, driven by their unwavering commitment and the resilience that characterizes their profession.

While caregiving can be arduous, the rewards it offers are immeasurable. The bonds formed between caregivers and those they care for transcend words, creating a profound sense of fulfillment and purpose. Witnessing even small improvements in the well-being of their charges brings an unparalleled sense of accomplishment. The gratitude expressed by patients, their families, and the broader community amplifies the value of a caregiver's efforts. Caregivers find solace in knowing that their compassionate actions contribute to the comfort, dignity, and happiness of those they serve, leaving a lasting positive impact on lives.

The influence of caregivers extends far beyond the individuals directly in their care. The compassionate energy they radiate creates a ripple effect that resonates through families, communities, and society as a whole. Their example inspires others to adopt a mindset of kindness and empathy. The support caregivers offer can enable families to remain united, as they navigate challenging circumstances together. Additionally, the care and attention provided by caregivers can alleviate burdens on healthcare systems and contribute to a more compassionate and connected society.

Caregivers are the unsung heroes who illuminate the path of human connection with their unwavering compassion and selflessness. Their role is a testament to the power of empathy, kindness, and dedication to making the world a better place for those in need. The challenges they face are overshadowed by the profound impact they have on the lives they touch, fostering resilience, hope, and healing. The journey of a caregiver is a testament to the transformative power of caring for others, underscoring the human potential for empathy and compassion, and reminding us all that in the tapestry of humanity, every thread of care weaves a brighter, more connected world.

Mastering Climate Control:
Navigating HVAC Realms as
a Skilled Technician

In the modern world, where climate control is essential for both residential and commercial spaces, HVAC technicians emerge as unsung heroes. This section explores the multifaceted role of an HVAC technician, delving into their responsibilities, the skills they possess, and the impact they have on ensuring comfortable and healthy environments. From installation to maintenance and repair, HVAC technicians play a pivotal role in maintaining indoor air quality and creating spaces where occupants can thrive.

HVAC technicians are responsible for creating and maintaining optimal indoor climates. Their duties encompass a wide range of tasks, starting from installing heating, ventilation, and air conditioning systems to ensuring their efficient operation. They inspect systems, diagnose issues, perform repairs, and conduct routine maintenance to ensure proper functioning. Additionally, HVAC technicians often advise clients on energy-efficient practices and recommend system upgrades to enhance performance and reduce environmental impact.

The role of an HVAC technician demands a diverse skill set that combines technical expertise with interpersonal abilities. Technical skills include a deep understanding of thermodynamics, refrigeration principles, electrical systems, and diagnostics. Proficiency in reading blueprints and technical manuals is essential for installation and repair tasks. Interpersonal qualities, such as effective communication and problem-solving, enable HVAC technicians to interact with clients, explain complex concepts, and address concerns.

HVAC technicians face a blend of challenges that stem from the complexity of systems they work with and the changing nature of technology. As buildings become more energy-efficient and environmentally conscious, technicians must adapt to new equipment and regulations. Moreover, working in extreme temperatures and confined spaces can be physically demanding. Despite these challenges, the rewards are significant. HVAC technicians contribute to creating comfortable and safe environments, improving air quality, and ensuring optimal system efficiency.

Becoming a skilled HVAC technician requires a combination of formal education, hands-on training, and continuous learning. Many technicians attend trade schools or community colleges to earn degrees or certifications in HVAC technology. Apprenticeships provide invaluable practical experience under the guidance of experienced technicians. Given the evolving nature of HVAC technology and energy-efficient practices, ongoing professional development is crucial for technicians to stay current and proficient.

The work of HVAC technicians resonates far beyond the mechanical systems they install and repair. Their efforts contribute to creating healthy indoor environments that promote well-being, productivity, and comfort. By ensuring proper ventilation and air filtration, HVAC technicians play a key role in preventing indoor air pollution and the spread of airborne illnesses. In commercial spaces, efficient HVAC systems contribute to employee satisfaction and customer experience. Ultimately, the work of HVAC technicians aligns with broader societal goals of sustainability and quality of life.

HVAC technicians are the backbone of modern comfort, enabling people to live and work in spaces tailored to their needs. Their role combines technical mastery with problem-solving prowess, ensuring that indoor environments remain comfortable, healthy, and efficient. As they navigate challenges, acquire new skills, and adapt to changing technologies, HVAC technicians play an indispensable role in shaping the quality of

Evidence and Empathy: Navigating the World as a Trauma and Crime Scene Specialist

In the aftermath of tragic events, there exists a profession that undertakes the challenging task of restoring spaces marred by trauma. Trauma Scene Remediation Specialists are the unsung heroes who clean and decontaminate scenes affected by traumatic incidents, providing a critical service that goes beyond the physical realm. Their work not only involves technical expertise in cleaning hazardous materials but also requires a profound understanding of the emotional impact these scenes can have on individuals and communities. This section explores the multifaceted world of Trauma Scene Remediation Specialists, delving into their essential role, the emotional toll of their work, the importance of compassion, and the healing they bring to those affected.

Trauma Scene Remediation Specialists play a pivotal role in restoring environments affected by various traumatic incidents, including suicides, homicides, accidents, and other critical events. Their expertise is essential in safely and effectively cleaning and decontaminating biohazardous materials, blood, bodily fluids, and other remnants of traumatic events. By meticulously removing these hazards, they help prevent potential health risks and ensure the safety of future occupants. The comprehensive cleaning process often involves not only visible contamination but also hidden traces that might carry biological risks. Their meticulous work contributes to the physical restoration of the space, allowing it to be repurposed and reclaimed.

The work of Trauma Scene Remediation Specialists extends beyond the tangible cleanup process; it intersects with the emotional aftermath of traumatic events. They enter spaces charged with grief, pain, and anguish, understanding that their actions are part of a healing process for the affected individuals and communities. Witnessing the aftermath of tragedies requires a high degree of emotional resilience and empathy. Specialists must delicately navigate these environments while recognizing the gravity of the situations. This emotional intelligence is a testament to their ability to balance technical skills with the human aspect of their work.

Compassion and sensitivity are cornerstones of a Trauma Scene Remediation Specialist's approach. Their interactions with victims' families, property owners, and first responders require a delicate balance between professionalism and empathy. Specialists often become a support system for those grappling with shock and grief, offering reassurance during moments of vulnerability. Demonstrating compassion in their interactions helps foster a sense of trust and understanding, creating an environment where affected individuals feel supported during a difficult time. This empathy-centered approach not only aids in the emotional healing process but also underscores the importance of human connection in times of crisis.

Trauma Scene Remediation Specialists are envoys of healing through restoration. Their work transcends the physical realm, permeating into the emotional and psychological spaces of those affected by trauma. By restoring scenes to their pre-incident state, these specialists offer a sense of closure and renewal. Their meticulous efforts not only contribute to the safety of the environment but also aid in the emotional recovery of individuals and communities. The act of restoring a space allows survivors and loved ones to move forward without the constant visual reminder of the trauma. In this way, Trauma Scene Remediation Specialists provide a unique form of healing through their commitment to comprehensive restoration.

Trauma Scene Remediation Specialists occupy a unique and essential niche in the aftermath of traumatic events.

Their work combines technical expertise, emotional resilience, compassion, and a commitment to healing. By addressing the physical remnants of trauma, they contribute to the restoration of environments and offer a path towards emotional recovery. These specialists embody the intersection of practicality and empathy, standing as beacons of hope in the midst of darkness. As silent healers, they play an integral role in helping communities and individuals navigate the aftermath of trauma and find solace in the process of restoration.

Sanitation Heroes: The Unseen World of Portable Toilet Cleaning

In the realm of sanitation and public health, a group of dedicated individuals plays a vital yet often overlooked role – portable toilet cleaners. These unsung heroes are entrusted with the task of maintaining the cleanliness and hygiene of portable toilets, ensuring the comfort and well-being of countless individuals in various public events, construction sites, and outdoor gatherings. The profession of a portable toilet cleaner goes beyond mere cleaning; it encompasses challenges, skills, and a sense of responsibility that contribute to the overall public health and sanitation. This section dives into the multifaceted world of portable toilet cleaners, exploring their role in promoting hygiene, their impact on events and communities, their daily challenges, and the sense of satisfaction that drives their work.

The role of a portable toilet cleaner is intrinsically linked to public health and hygiene. These professionals are tasked with maintaining facilities that offer a clean and safe option for individuals who lack access to traditional restroom facilities. By keeping portable toilets sanitary and well-maintained, cleaners contribute to the prevention of the spread of diseases and the maintenance of overall public health. In environments where large crowds gather, such as festivals, outdoor events, and construction sites, the proper management of waste and sanitation is essential. Portable toilet cleaners ensure that attendees and workers have access to facilities that are not only functional but also hygienic.

Portable toilet cleaners have a significant impact on the success of events and the overall experience of attendees. In events ranging from music festivals to outdoor weddings, the availability of clean and well-maintained portable toilets contributes to the comfort and satisfaction of participants.

Clean facilities enhance the overall event atmosphere, allowing attendees to focus on enjoying the experience rather than worrying about sanitation. Moreover, in construction sites and remote locations, portable toilet cleaners provide essential services to workers, ensuring their well-being and efficiency. Their behind-the-scenes contributions play a vital role in the smooth operation of events and the functionality of work sites.

The profession of a portable toilet cleaner comes with its share of challenges that demand specialized skills and adaptability. Cleaners often work in various weather conditions, from scorching heat to pouring rain, which requires physical resilience and dedication. The efficient removal, treatment, and disposal of waste materials involve technical knowledge and the use of appropriate equipment. Portable toilet cleaners must also adhere to stringent health and safety regulations to ensure that the facilities are both sanitary and environmentally responsible. Their expertise extends beyond simple cleaning to the proper handling of waste and the maintenance of equipment to prevent breakdowns.

Despite the challenges, portable toilet cleaners find a sense of satisfaction in their work, knowing that they play a crucial role in maintaining public health and hygiene. The tangible impact of their efforts can be seen in the comfort of event attendees and workers. Providing clean facilities that contribute to the overall positive experience of people gives cleaners a sense of accomplishment. This feeling of contribution extends to the communities they serve, as their work directly influences the well-being of individuals in various contexts. This sense of responsibility and contribution fuels their dedication to a profession that often goes unnoticed by the public.

The role of a portable toilet cleaner extends beyond the surface-level task of cleaning facilities; it is a vital part of promoting public health, enhancing events, and supporting communities. These professionals operate behind the scenes, ensuring that sanitation remains a top priority in various settings. Their dedication to maintaining clean and functional portable toilets is a testament to their commitment to public welfare. As unsung heroes, portable toilet cleaners deserve recognition for their integral role in ensuring the comfort and hygiene of individuals attending events, working on construction sites, or navigating other outdoor spaces. Their unassuming work serves as a reminder of the significance of even the most understated professions in upholding the standards of sanitation and well-being.

Beyond the Bin: Navigating the World as a Waste Management Technician

Amidst the urban hustle and bustle, a group of dedicated individuals quietly shoulders the responsibility of keeping our surroundings clean and hygienic. Waste Management Technicians, often referred to as "garbage collectors" or "sanitation workers," play a vital yet often underrated role in maintaining public health and the environment. Their work involves collecting, sorting, and disposing of waste, ensuring the proper management of trash and recyclables. This section explores into the multifaceted world of Waste Management Technicians, exploring their contribution to public health, environmental sustainability, the challenges they face, the expertise they possess, and the dignity of their often-unnoticed labor.

The work of Waste Management Technicians directly impacts public health by preventing the spread of diseases and maintaining a clean environment. The proper disposal of waste minimizes the risk of vermin infestations, contamination of water sources, and the proliferation of harmful pathogens. In urban areas, the efficient collection and disposal of garbage contribute to curbing the spread of illnesses and fostering hygienic living conditions. Waste Management Technicians are the unsung heroes who work diligently to ensure that our communities remain safe and free from the health hazards associated with improper waste disposal.

In an era marked by increasing environmental awareness, Waste Management Technicians are at the forefront of the sustainability movement. By sorting and separating recyclables from regular waste, they contribute to reducing the strain on landfills and promoting the recycling loop. Their work directly impacts the conservation of natural resources and the reduction of greenhouse gas emissions associated with waste decomposition. Waste Management Technicians play a critical role in implementing waste reduction strategies, encouraging communities to adopt responsible waste disposal practices, and contributing to a cleaner, greener future for generations to come.

The work of Waste Management Technicians is not without challenges. They face exposure to varying weather conditions, heavy lifting, and the need to operate heavy machinery. The physically demanding nature of the job requires a high level of physical fitness and the ability to adapt to different scenarios. Moreover, their expertise goes beyond the collection and disposal of waste; they are knowledgeable about recycling protocols, hazardous waste handling, and safety regulations. Their understanding of waste management systems allows them to make informed decisions about sorting, transportation, and disposal, ensuring that waste is managed in the most responsible and environmentally conscious manner.

Waste Management Technicians exemplify the dignity of labor. Their work, though often unnoticed, is essential to the functioning of our communities. They maintain the orderliness of our neighborhoods, contribute to public health, and uphold the principles of sustainability. Despite the challenges they face, Waste Management Technicians take pride in their roles as guardians of cleanliness. Their efforts create a sense of accomplishment, knowing that their work has a tangible impact on the well-being of the people they serve.

While their work may go unnoticed by many, Waste Management Technicians often foster a unique connection with the communities they serve. They become familiar faces in neighborhoods, developing relationships with residents and local businesses. Their interactions with community members go beyond the collection of waste; they share tips on responsible disposal, offer guidance on recycling practices, and provide a sense of reassurance that the community's well-being is in capable hands. As communities increasingly recognize the importance of waste management, there is a growing movement to acknowledge and appreciate the efforts of Waste Management Technicians, highlighting their indispensable role.

Waste Management Technicians stand as the backbone of cleanliness and sanitation in our communities. Their diligent efforts contribute to public health, environmental sustainability, and the overall quality of life. As the world grapples with waste management challenges, their role becomes even more crucial. These unsung heroes embody the values of responsibility, dedication, and dignity in labor. As we reflect on the impact of their work, we recognize that Waste Management Technicians are more than just collectors of waste; they are the guardians of our surroundings, the stewards of our health, and the champions of a cleaner, more sustainable future.

Beneath the Earth's Veins:
Journeying into the Depths
as a Coal Miner

In the annals of industrial history, the role of a coal miner stands as a testament to both the challenges and the vital contributions that shape societies. Coal miners venture deep into the earth's crust, navigating through dark and treacherous passages to extract coal, a resource that has powered civilizations for centuries. Beyond the physical demands, being a coal miner is a way of life that combines courage, camaraderie, and resilience. This section adventures into the intricate world of coal miners, exploring their grueling work conditions, the camaraderie that develops underground, the historical significance of coal mining, the risks they face, and their indelible contribution to global progress.

Coal mining is synonymous with arduous labor conducted in some of the most challenging environments. Miners toil in subterranean chambers, often facing poor ventilation, limited space, and extreme temperatures. The physical demands include heavy lifting, drilling, and the constant threat of cave-ins and gas leaks. Despite these harsh conditions, a unique camaraderie develops among coal miners. The shared challenges and reliance on each other's skills form a bond that transcends words. This camaraderie creates a sense of unity, where each miner's well-being depends on the collective effort of the team. In the darkness below, trust and cooperation become pillars of survival and success.

Coal mining has played a pivotal role in shaping the course of human history and industrial development. The extraction of coal fueled the Industrial Revolution, powering factories, trains, and the expansion of economies worldwide. Coal miners became the backbone of progress, enabling societies to leap into the modern age. Their labor provided the energy needed to transform raw materials into finished goods, propelling economies into new realms of production and consumption. While coal's prominence has diminished in recent years due to environmental concerns, the historical significance of coal miners remains an integral part of the global narrative of progress.

The life of a coal miner is fraught with risks that underscore their dedication and bravery. Cave-ins, gas explosions, black lung disease, and other hazards loom ominously in the darkness. Despite stringent safety regulations, coal mining remains one of the most dangerous occupations. Miners work in an environment where the potential for disaster is ever-present. The risks extend not only to their physical well-being but also to their mental and emotional health. The constant awareness of danger weighs heavily on miners and their families, forming a backdrop of sacrifice that often goes unnoticed by the wider world.

The legacy of coal miners is one of resilience and unwavering dedication. They have endured extreme conditions, faced life-threatening risks, and contributed significantly to the growth of economies and societies. Their labor has powered progress, bridging the gap between eras and cultures. The sweat and sacrifice of coal miners have created foundations for the modern world, demonstrating the spirit of tenacity that defines the human experience. While coal mining's environmental implications have sparked calls for change, the contributions of coal miners to global development remain an integral part of history's tapestry.

The life of a coal miner is a paradox, characterized by both the darkness of the earth's depths and the brilliance of their contributions to global progress. Their work involves not only extracting coal but also embodying a legacy of resilience, camaraderie, and dedication. As we reflect on the sacrifices and challenges faced by coal miners, we acknowledge their role in shaping the world's trajectory. From the Industrial Revolution to the present day, coal miners have stood as pillars of progress, their labor a testament to the potential of human determination. Their story is one of endurance, unity, and the enduring pursuit of light in the darkness below.

Guardians of Waste: Navigating the Terrain as a Landfill Operator

In the realm of waste management, a group of dedicated professionals known as landfill operators stand as the guardians of responsible waste disposal. Operating at the interface of human consumption and environmental impact, landfill operators play a vital role in managing the waste generated by societies. Their work involves overseeing the operation, maintenance, and compliance of landfill sites – repositories of discarded materials that must be managed with utmost care. This section delves into the intricate world of landfill operators, exploring their responsibilities, environmental stewardship, challenges they face, technological advancements, and their role in creating a more sustainable future.

Landfill operators bear the immense responsibility of managing waste disposal sites, ensuring that waste is collected, compacted, and covered in a manner that minimizes its impact on the environment. They are responsible for preventing contamination of soil and water sources, reducing methane emissions – a potent greenhouse gas – and adhering to strict environmental regulations. Landfill operators serve as environmental stewards, working diligently to strike a balance between waste management and the preservation of natural ecosystems. Their work extends beyond waste containment; it involves creating systems that minimize environmental degradation while efficiently managing waste streams.

Operating a landfill comes with a myriad of challenges that require adaptability and expertise. Landfill operators must manage various waste types, from household trash to hazardous materials, each requiring specific handling and disposal methods. They navigate logistical challenges such as waste transportation, resource allocation, and site optimization. Moreover, the management of public perceptions and concerns about landfills requires effective communication skills and community engagement. With the increasing emphasis on sustainability, landfill operators are faced with the challenge of implementing innovative waste management strategies that minimize the landfill's footprint and explore alternatives to traditional disposal methods.

In the age of technological advancement, the role of landfill operators has evolved to incorporate cutting-edge solutions for waste management. Landfills are no longer mere dumping grounds; they are equipped with advanced systems to capture and utilize methane gas for energy generation. Operators use technology to monitor landfill gas emissions, leachate levels, and overall site conditions in real-time, allowing for prompt intervention and optimal waste management. Technological tools aid in optimizing waste compaction, tracking waste movement, and assessing environmental impacts, transforming landfills into dynamic, controlled environments that minimize their effect on surrounding ecosystems.

Landfill operators play a critical role in steering waste management practices toward sustainability. By adhering to best practices and embracing innovative technologies, they contribute to the reduction of greenhouse gas emissions, the preservation of natural resources, and the advancement of a circular economy. Landfills are evolving from mere disposal sites to hubs of resource recovery, with operators actively participating in efforts to extract value from waste through recycling, composting, and energy generation. The work of landfill operators is integral to shaping waste management practices that align with global environmental goals, contributing to a cleaner, more sustainable future.

Landfill operators hold a unique position at the nexus of waste and environmental responsibility. Their work encompasses much more than waste containment; it involves environmental stewardship, technological innovation, and a commitment to creating a more sustainable world. As guardians of waste management, landfill operators are entrusted with the challenge of minimizing the negative impact of waste on the environment while harnessing its potential for resource recovery. Their efforts are a testament to the complex balance between consumption and conservation, embodying the pursuit of responsible waste management and the collective responsibility of humanity toward the planet.

Life on the Edge: Navigating the High Seas as an Oil Rig Worker

Amidst the vast expanse of the open sea, a unique breed of individuals undertakes the daunting task of extracting a precious resource that fuels the modern world – oil. Oil rig workers, also known as "roughnecks," face the relentless waves, harsh weather, and the challenges of working in a confined, high-pressure environment. Their work is not just a job; it's a way of life that requires resilience, technical expertise, and camaraderie. This section dives into the intricate world of oil rig workers, exploring their roles in the energy sector, the adversities they overcome, the bonds they forge, the significance of their labor, and the future of their industry.

Oil rig workers play a pivotal role in the energy sector, where oil is a driving force for economies, industries, and transportation. These skilled individuals operate in the offshore and onshore environments, working tirelessly to extract crude oil from beneath the earth's surface. Their efforts contribute to meeting the world's energy demands, powering homes, vehicles, and industries. Oil rig workers form the backbone of oil exploration and drilling, making it possible to harness this invaluable resource that powers global progress.

The life of an oil rig worker is characterized by its inherent adversities. Offshore environments expose them to unpredictable weather patterns, relentless waves, and extreme temperatures. The isolation from the mainland, often for weeks or months at a time, can be mentally challenging. Additionally, the very nature of the work poses physical risks, as the machinery, equipment, and processes involved require careful attention and adherence to strict safety protocols. Despite these challenges, oil rig workers remain committed to their tasks, driven by the understanding of the importance of their labor and the sense of camaraderie that binds them.

The camaraderie among oil rig workers is a cornerstone of their profession. Living and working in close quarters for extended periods fosters a sense of community that transcends the confines of the rig. Workers rely on each other for safety, success, and support. The shared challenges, triumphs, and moments of downtime create an unbreakable bond that forms the foundation of their work culture. This camaraderie extends beyond the professional realm, resulting in friendships that last long after the rig assignments have ended.

The labor of oil rig workers extends far beyond the confines of the rig itself. Their efforts drive economic growth, ensure energy security, and maintain the intricate web of industries that rely on oil-derived products. From transportation to manufacturing, oil plays an indispensable role in modern life. The dedication of oil rig workers to extract this resource efficiently and responsibly speaks to the magnitude of their contribution to the global economy. Their work allows societies to function, industries to thrive, and progress to continue unhindered.

As the world shifts towards sustainable and renewable energy sources, the future of oil rig workers is poised for transformation. The energy sector is undergoing a profound transition, with increased emphasis on clean energy solutions. Oil rig workers are faced with the challenge of adapting their skills to new technologies, diversifying their expertise, and participating in the evolving energy landscape. While the demand for oil remains, the industry is embracing innovation and sustainability. The resilience and adaptability that define oil rig workers will serve them well as they navigate this transformation.

Oil rig workers epitomize the tenacity and determination required to extract a vital resource from the depths of the sea. Their labor fuels economies, industries, and innovations that shape the modern world. Beyond the physical challenges, oil rig workers exemplify camaraderie, forging bonds that transcend the confines of the rig. As the energy sector evolves, they stand ready to adapt, embracing new technologies and sustainability measures. The legacy of oil rig workers is one of resilience, unity, and their indispensable role in powering the global engine of progress.

Elevating Expertise: Navigating Heights as an Elevator Repairer

In the modern urban landscape, where towering skyscrapers define city skylines, the role of an elevator repairer takes on a pivotal significance. These skilled professionals are the unsung heroes behind the seamless vertical transportation that millions rely on daily. Elevator repairers, often working at great heights and under demanding conditions, ensure the safety, efficiency, and reliability of elevators and escalators. Their job involves a unique blend of technical expertise, problem-solving, and commitment to public safety. This section explores into the intricate world of elevator repairers, exploring the complexities of their work, the challenges they face, the crucial role they play in urban infrastructure, the advancements in elevator technology, and their contribution to modern society.

Elevator repairers are craftsmen in the realm of modern technology. Their work requires an intricate understanding of the complex mechanical and electrical systems that power elevators and escalators. From hydraulic lifts to high-speed traction systems, elevator repairers diagnose issues, troubleshoot malfunctions, and perform intricate repairs. Their expertise extends to safety mechanisms, computer controls, and intricate wiring. This technical mastery ensures that elevators operate seamlessly, contributing to the smooth functioning of high-rise buildings and the convenience of urban life.

Elevator repairers embrace the challenges of working at significant heights, often scaling the heights of towering structures to access equipment and machinery. These heights come with their own set of challenges, including vertigo-inducing views, unpredictable weather, and the need for precision work while suspended in the air. The courage to operate in these conditions is a testament to the dedication of elevator repairers to their craft. Their work often goes unnoticed by the public, but the smooth, safe rides in elevators owe much to their skillful interventions high above the ground.

The role of elevator repairers is integral to the urban infrastructure that defines modern cities. Elevators are lifelines within skyscrapers, providing efficient vertical transportation for office workers, residents, and visitors alike. Without properly functioning elevators, the functionality of high-rise buildings would be severely compromised. Elevator repairers ensure that buildings remain operational, safe, and compliant with regulations. Their work impacts every sector of urban life, from commerce to hospitality, healthcare to residential living.

As technology advances, elevators continue to evolve, and so do the responsibilities of elevator repairers. The integration of smart technology, energy-efficient systems, and digital controls has transformed elevators from mechanical marvels to sophisticated technological wonders. Elevator repairers now work with state-of-the-art diagnostics, remote monitoring, and predictive maintenance tools. Their role extends beyond fixing malfunctions; they actively participate in implementing cutting-edge solutions that enhance efficiency, reduce energy consumption, and improve user experience.

Elevator repairers contribute to the fabric of modern society in profound ways. Their work ensures that buildings remain accessible to all, regardless of mobility challenges. They create environments that facilitate the movement of people, fostering inclusivity and efficiency. Elevator repairers are the enablers of urban living, providing the infrastructure that allows people to live and work at elevated heights. Their technical prowess ensures that the marvels of modern architecture remain functional and safe, enriching the lives of individuals across the globe.

Elevator repairers are the hidden architects of vertical transportation, contributing to the seamless movement of individuals within urban landscapes. Their technical mastery, willingness to tackle heights, and commitment to safety underscore their invaluable role. In an era of technological innovation, elevator repairers adapt to new challenges, ensuring that elevators remain cutting-edge and efficient. Their work touches the lives of millions, from office workers to tourists, residents to healthcare providers. Elevator repairers elevate more than just physical structures; they elevate the very essence of modern society, providing the means for people to reach new heights – both literally and metaphorically.

Preserving Memories: Navigating
the World of Embalming
with Compassion

In the realm of end-of-life care, a unique profession exists that combines artistry, science, and compassion – that of an embalmer. These skilled individuals play a crucial role in preparing the deceased for their final farewell, ensuring that the departed are presented with dignity and respect. Embalmers, often working behind the scenes, are entrusted with the delicate task of preserving and preparing the deceased for viewing by loved ones. This section adventures into the multifaceted world of embalmers, exploring the significance of their work, the emotional toll it takes, the technical expertise involved, the role they play in the grieving process, and the lasting impact of their contributions.

Embalming is a practice that dates back centuries and is deeply rooted in cultural and religious customs. Embalmers are responsible for gently preserving the body, temporarily halting the natural processes of decomposition. This allows family and friends to have a final opportunity to say goodbye in a peaceful and respectful environment. Beyond the preservation of the physical body, embalmers contribute to creating lasting memories for the bereaved. Their work allows loved ones to remember the deceased as they were in life, providing a sense of closure and comfort during a time of profound loss.

While embalmers are skilled professionals, their work is accompanied by emotional challenges. They often interact closely with grieving families, witnessing their pain and sorrow firsthand. The ability to approach their work with compassion, empathy, and sensitivity is crucial. Embalmers not only preserve the physical remains but also offer emotional support to families during an emotionally charged period. Their ability to navigate the fine line between professionalism and human connection is a testament to their dedication to both their craft and the individuals they serve.

Embalming is a complex and delicate process that requires technical expertise and a keen eye for detail. Embalmers are well-versed in anatomy, chemistry, and various embalming techniques. They use a combination of fluids, instruments, and techniques to preserve the body while maintaining a natural appearance. Embalmers also use their artistic skills to ensure that the deceased looks peaceful and serene, helping to create a positive memory for loved ones. Their work involves a delicate balance of science and artistry, where precision and aesthetics intertwine to achieve a final result that honors the individual's unique identity.

Embalmers play an integral role in the grieving process, offering families the opportunity to say goodbye and find solace in their loss. The act of viewing the deceased can provide a sense of closure, allowing family and friends to acknowledge the reality of the passing and find a measure of comfort in the midst of grief. Embalmers contribute to creating an environment that fosters healing and reflection. By enabling families to see their loved ones one last time, embalmers provide an invaluable service that aids in the emotional journey of acceptance and mourning.

The work of embalmers extends beyond the immediate preparation of the deceased; it leaves a lasting impact on the memories of those left behind. The serene and dignified presentation of the body during a viewing or funeral service creates a memory that lingers in the hearts of family and friends. Embalmers contribute to the collective experience of grief, enabling individuals to process their emotions and celebrate the life of the departed. Through their careful work, embalmers offer a space for healing, connection, and remembrance.

The role of an embalmer encompasses more than just

the technical aspects of preparing the deceased for final rites. It is a profession rooted in compassion, respect, and the human experience of loss. Embalmers are the silent guardians of memories, ensuring that the final moments of a person's physical presence are marked by dignity and grace. Their work aids in the healing process and allows individuals to find solace in the midst of sorrow. Embalmers are both artists and caretakers, guiding families through a delicate and emotional journey, and leaving an indelible mark on the memories of those they serve.

Guiding Farewells: The Compassionate Journey of a Mortician

Amidst the delicate transition between life and death, a profession of great significance emerges – that of a mortician. Often working behind the scenes, morticians are entrusted with the intricate task of providing compassionate care to the deceased and supporting grieving families during their most vulnerable moments. Their role extends beyond the technical aspects of preparing bodies for burial; it involves offering solace, honoring the departed, and guiding families through the grieving process. This section delves into the multifaceted world of morticians, exploring their unique role, the emotional and ethical considerations they navigate, the skills they possess, the impact of their work on families, and the enduring legacy they create.

Morticians serve as compassionate guides for families navigating the complex process of arranging funerals and memorial services. Their role extends beyond the realm of preparing bodies; it involves helping families make informed decisions, coordinating logistics, and providing emotional support. Morticians understand that the grieving process is deeply personal and unique for each family, and they offer a steady hand to guide families through the myriad choices they face during a difficult time. Their presence is a source of comfort, ensuring that the memory of the departed is honored with dignity and respect.

The work of a mortician demands a delicate balance between emotional sensitivity and ethical responsibility. Morticians must remain attuned to the emotions of grieving families while ensuring that the body is treated with the utmost care and reverence. They approach their work with empathy, understanding that every individual and family has a unique story that deserves to be acknowledged. Additionally, morticians adhere to strict ethical guidelines, maintaining transparency, honesty, and integrity in their interactions with families. Their ability to navigate these complex considerations is a testament to their dedication to both the deceased and the families they serve.

Morticians possess a diverse range of skills that go beyond the technical aspects of their work. They are adept at communication, offering a listening ear to grieving families and creating an environment of trust. Their organizational skills ensure that all logistical aspects of a funeral or memorial service run smoothly. Furthermore, their expertise in embalming, body preparation, and restoration ensures that the deceased is presented in a dignified and natural manner. Morticians are knowledgeable about legal requirements, cultural customs, and religious practices, allowing them to tailor their services to the unique needs of each family.

Morticians play an integral role in the healing process of grieving families. By providing a supportive environment, they enable families to focus on their emotional journey without the burden of logistical details. The care and respect shown by morticians toward the deceased can offer comfort and solace to families as they bid their final farewells. Additionally, the collaborative efforts of morticians and families in planning memorial services contribute to the creation of meaningful tributes that celebrate the life of the departed. The legacy of a loved one is honored through the compassionate work of morticians, leaving a lasting impact on the memories of those left behind.

The work of morticians extends far beyond the physical act of preparing bodies; it is about honoring the lives that have been lived and the memories that remain. Morticians create an enduring legacy by facilitating a meaningful and respectful transition from life to death. The care and attention they offer to both the deceased and the bereaved families contribute to a sense of closure and healing. The impact of their work ripples through generations, as families remember the dignified farewell their loved ones received and the support they found during a time of profound loss.

The role of a mortician is one of profound significance, encompassing compassion, empathy, and skillful guidance. Morticians are the silent pillars of support for grieving families, offering solace during moments of vulnerability and facilitating the process of saying goodbye. Their work goes beyond the technical aspects of their craft; it is about nurturing the healing process and creating lasting memories. As they navigate the delicate balance between emotions and ethics, morticians play a vital role in helping families honor the lives of their loved ones and find a sense of closure. In the tapestry of life and death, morticians weave threads of compassion and respect, leaving an indelible mark on the hearts of those they serve.

Hidden Realities: Exploring the
Depths as a Sewage Inspector

Beneath the bustling urban landscapes lies an intricate network that is often overlooked yet crucial to public health and environmental well-being – the sewage system. Sewage inspectors are the unsung heroes who navigate this hidden world to ensure the proper functioning of waste disposal systems. Their work involves investigating, assessing, and maintaining sewage systems, safeguarding communities from health hazards and environmental degradation. This section dives into the vital world of sewage inspectors, exploring the significance of their role, the challenges they encounter, the expertise they possess, their contributions to public health, and their role in creating a cleaner, safer world.

Sewage inspectors hold a critical role in maintaining the health and safety of communities. They monitor and inspect sewage systems to ensure that waste is being properly collected, transported, and treated. By identifying potential issues and ensuring compliance with regulations, sewage inspectors prevent contamination of water sources, soil, and the spread of diseases. Their work is instrumental in preventing public health crises and environmental disasters that could arise from the improper management of sewage. In essence, sewage inspectors contribute to the foundation of community well-being that often goes unnoticed.

Navigating the world of sewage inspection is not for the faint of heart. Sewage inspectors must face unpleasant and hazardous conditions, working in confined spaces, often exposed to foul odors and hazardous materials. The environment they work in can be physically demanding, requiring agility and resilience. Moreover, sewage inspectors must remain vigilant about safety protocols to minimize the risk of exposure to harmful substances. Their ability to operate under these challenging conditions reflects their dedication to safeguarding public health and environmental integrity.

Sewage inspectors are experts in understanding the complex infrastructure that comprises sewage systems. They possess in-depth knowledge of plumbing, wastewater treatment processes, and the regulatory framework governing waste disposal. Their technical mastery allows them to identify potential issues, from blockages to leaks, and to recommend appropriate solutions. Moreover, their expertise extends to maintaining accurate records, conducting thorough inspections, and communicating findings effectively to local authorities, ensuring that corrective actions are taken promptly.

The work of sewage inspectors has far-reaching implications for public health and the environment. By preventing sewage system failures and identifying issues early on, they minimize the risk of disease outbreaks and water contamination. Clean and functional sewage systems protect the ecosystem, preserving water quality and preventing the degradation of soil and aquatic habitats. The contributions of sewage inspectors extend beyond their technical tasks; they actively contribute to the betterment of communities, ensuring that residents have access to safe and sanitary living conditions.

Sewage inspectors play an essential role in creating a cleaner, safer world for present and future generations. Their work aligns with broader environmental goals, such as promoting sustainable waste management practices and minimizing the impact of human activities on natural resources. By enforcing regulations and maintaining the integrity of sewage systems, sewage inspectors actively contribute to environmental conservation and the well-being of ecosystems. Their efforts resonate with the larger movement toward responsible stewardship of the planet.

Sewage inspectors may work in the unseen realm, but their impact on public health and the environment is undeniable. Their dedication to safeguarding communities from potential health hazards and environmental degradation reflects a commitment to the greater good. Sewage inspectors are the silent sentinels, ensuring that the hidden infrastructure that supports modern life functions smoothly and safely. As we reflect on their role, we acknowledge that they contribute not only to the prevention of crises but also to the preservation of the planet's health. Their work embodies the principle that true heroes operate behind the scenes, making a profound difference in the world we live in.

Silent Vigilance: Life on the Night
Shift as a Security Guard

In an increasingly complex and interconnected world, security guards serve as the unsung heroes who safeguard our communities, establishments, and valuable assets. This section delves into the multifaceted role of a security guard, shedding light on the responsibilities they shoulder, the skills they wield, and the challenges they face. From maintaining a watchful eye on premises to handling emergency situations, security guards play a pivotal role in upholding safety and order.

Security guards serve as the first line of defense against potential threats to individuals and property. Their duties encompass a wide range of tasks, including patrolling premises, monitoring surveillance systems, and controlling access to restricted areas. Through their vigilant presence, security guards deter criminal activity and unauthorized access, fostering a secure environment for employees, visitors, and residents. Additionally, they often provide customer service by offering directions, answering questions, and guiding individuals during emergencies.

The role of a security guard demands a blend of technical skills, interpersonal abilities, and a strong moral compass. Technical skills include operating security systems, understanding emergency protocols, and administering first aid when necessary. Interpersonal skills are equally crucial, as security guards must communicate effectively with diverse groups of people, diffuse potentially tense situations, and collaborate with law enforcement when required. Furthermore, integrity, resilience, and adaptability are qualities that enable security guards to navigate unexpected challenges and maintain their professionalism under pressure.

Despite the critical nature of their work, security guards encounter various challenges that can test their mettle. One challenge is the unpredictability of their environment, which exposes them to potential dangers such as theft, vandalism, and confrontations with aggressive individuals. Moreover, long shifts and irregular hours can lead to fatigue and affect their alertness, potentially compromising their effectiveness. In some instances, security guards may also face skepticism from the public or perceive a lack of recognition for their contributions, which can impact their morale.

To address the complex challenges of their role, security guards undergo rigorous training and continuous professional development. Training programs cover topics such as emergency response procedures, conflict resolution, and legal guidelines to ensure guards are equipped to handle various scenarios. Additionally, advancements in technology require guards to stay updated with the latest security systems and tools. Professional development opportunities not only enhance their skills but also empower them to take on leadership roles within the security industry.

The presence of security guards goes beyond mere protection; it fosters a sense of safety and tranquility within communities and establishments. Schools, malls, corporate offices, and residential complexes all benefit from the watchful eyes of security guards, as their vigilant stance deters criminal behavior and promotes an environment conducive to productivity and well-being. Their efforts contribute to a positive quality of life by safeguarding both tangible assets and intangible peace of mind.

In the intricate tapestry of modern society, security guards stand as stalwart sentinels, fulfilling a multifaceted role that demands a combination of technical skills, interpersonal finesse, and unwavering dedication. Their duties extend beyond safeguarding assets; they create safe spaces where individuals can thrive without the fear of harm. While challenges may abound, the impact of security guards on communities is undeniable, making their role an essential cornerstone of our collective security and well-being.

Sculpting Success: Guiding Fitness Journeys as a Personal Trainer

In a world where health and fitness have taken center stage, personal trainers serve as catalysts for positive change in individuals' lives. This section explores the multifaceted role of a personal trainer, delving into their responsibilities, the skills they employ, and the impact they have on their clients' physical and mental well-being. From designing personalized workout plans to providing motivation and education, personal trainers play a crucial role in guiding individuals toward healthier lifestyles.

Personal trainers are much more than fitness enthusiasts; they are educators, motivators, and partners in their clients' wellness journeys. Their responsibilities encompass tailoring exercise programs to clients' goals and fitness levels, providing guidance on proper form and technique, and tracking progress over time. Beyond the gym floor, personal trainers often offer nutritional advice and lifestyle recommendations to help clients achieve holistic health improvements. In doing so, they create a comprehensive approach that extends beyond the realm of exercise.

The role of a personal trainer requires a blend of technical skills and interpersonal qualities. Proficiency in exercise physiology, nutrition science, and anatomy equips trainers with the knowledge to design safe and effective workout plans. Additionally, excellent communication skills enable trainers to establish rapport with clients, listen to their needs, and provide clear instructions. Patience, empathy, and adaptability allow trainers to tailor their approaches to each client's unique circumstances and challenges, fostering a supportive and effective training environment.

While the rewards of being a personal trainer are numerous, the profession also comes with its share of challenges. Trainers often encounter clients with varying levels of commitment, motivation, and physical limitations. Crafting customized solutions that align with each client's goals and abilities demands creativity and adaptability. Moreover, personal trainers must stay updated with the latest fitness trends, research, and methodologies to provide evidence-based guidance. The rewards, however, are immeasurable—witnessing clients transform physically and mentally, and knowing that their guidance contributes to improved well-being, creates a deep sense of fulfillment.

Becoming a skilled personal trainer involves continuous education and professional development. Formal certifications from reputable organizations equip trainers with the foundational knowledge and skills required for the role. Beyond initial certifications, personal trainers often pursue specialized courses in areas such as corrective exercise, sports conditioning, and group fitness instruction. This commitment to ongoing learning ensures that trainers remain up-to-date with industry advancements and can cater to a diverse clientele effectively.

The influence of personal trainers extends far beyond the gym walls. They contribute to a society that values health and well-being by helping clients overcome obstacles, establish healthy habits, and achieve their fitness goals. Beyond physical transformations, personal trainers often play a vital role in boosting clients' self-esteem, confidence, and mental resilience. As clients experience positive changes in their bodies and overall wellness, they become inspired to make healthier choices in their daily lives, thereby creating a ripple effect that spreads across families and communities.

In the realm of health and fitness, personal trainers emerge as guides, educators, and motivators who foster positive change in individuals' lives. Their multifaceted role demands a combination of technical expertise, interpersonal finesse, and an unwavering commitment to their clients' well-being. As they navigate challenges and witness transformations, personal trainers contribute not only to the betterment of their clients but also to a society that values and prioritizes health.

Braving the Icy Depths: Life as a
Crab Fisherman on the High Seas

Amid the tempestuous waves of the open ocean, a breed of seafarers takes on the daunting task of harvesting one of the most sought-after delicacies from the depths – crabs. Crab fishermen, known for their courage and resilience, navigate treacherous waters in pursuit of their catch. Their work is characterized by long hours, dangerous conditions, and an unwavering commitment to the sea. This section explores into the challenging world of crab fishermen, exploring the significance of their role, the harsh realities they face, the camaraderie that develops at sea, their connection to maritime traditions, and their contribution to the seafood industry.

Crab fishermen are an integral part of the seafood industry, providing a coveted delicacy to consumers around the world. Their catch, often comprising species like king crab and snow crab, graces the tables of fine dining establishments and households alike. The work of crab fishermen supports local economies, sustains coastal communities, and contributes to the broader culinary landscape. Beyond their economic impact, crab fishermen connect people to the richness of the sea, offering a taste of the ocean's bounty and enhancing the gastronomic experiences of seafood enthusiasts.

The life of a crab fisherman is marked by its inherent challenges. Operating in some of the most unforgiving marine environments, crab fishermen battle icy waters, tumultuous seas, and extreme weather conditions. The physical demands of hauling heavy pots and navigating slippery decks demand strength and endurance. Long working hours, often spanning days or even weeks at sea, test their mental and physical stamina. Additionally, the ever-present risk of accidents and injuries looms large, making safety measures a top priority. The ability to navigate these harsh realities is a testament to the resilience and determination of crab fishermen.

The close-knit camaraderie that forms among crab fishermen is a defining aspect of their profession. The shared challenges, risks, and triumphs create a bond that transcends mere co-workers; they become a second family at sea. Working in close quarters for extended periods fosters a sense of unity and mutual reliance. The camaraderie extends to times of rest as well, where stories, laughter, and shared meals become a respite from the rigors of the job. This sense of community is essential for maintaining morale and teamwork, ensuring the collective success of the crew.

Crab fishermen are inheritors of rich maritime traditions that have been passed down through generations. The profession carries a sense of legacy, connecting modern-day fishermen to the seafaring heritage of their predecessors. The rituals, practices, and unwritten codes of conduct create a sense of continuity with the past. While technology has evolved the tools of the trade, the essence of crab fishing remains steeped in tradition, fostering a deep respect for the sea and its rhythms.

The contributions of crab fishermen extend far beyond the decks of their vessels. Their work supports an industry that provides nourishment, economic livelihoods, and cultural connections. The seafood industry relies on their dedication to supply a delicacy that has become a culinary staple. Crab fishermen play a pivotal role in maintaining seafood sustainability, adhering to regulations and best practices to ensure that crab populations remain abundant for future generations. Their commitment to responsible fishing practices safeguards the delicate balance of ocean ecosystems.

Crab fishermen embark on a journey fraught with challenges, bravery, and a deep connection to the sea. Their tireless efforts provide not only a culinary delight but also sustain communities and support maritime traditions. As we contemplate the hardships they endure, we recognize the vital role they play in the seafood industry and the broader fabric of coastal life. Crab fishermen are the guardians of a legacy that spans generations, combining the best of tradition and innovation as they navigate the treacherous waters in search of the ocean's treasures. In their pursuit, they embody the spirit of exploration, the resilience of seafaring, and the enduring bond between humanity and the sea.

Collecting the Roadway Toll:
Life in the Operator's Booth

As vehicles traverse the vast network of highways, bridges, and tunnels that crisscross our modern landscape, a crucial checkpoint stands between the open road and the destination – the toll booth. Behind the glass windows of these unassuming booths, toll booth operators perform a vital role in ensuring the smooth flow of traffic and the collection of toll fees. Often overlooked, these operators play a pivotal role in maintaining transportation infrastructure and facilitating the movement of goods and people. This section adventures into the life of a toll booth operator, exploring the significance of their role, the challenges they face, their interactions with travelers, the role they play in transportation funding, and their contribution to road safety.

Toll booth operators are the frontline custodians of transportation infrastructure, ensuring that vehicles pay the required toll fees for the use of roads, bridges, and tunnels. These fees fund the maintenance, expansion, and enhancement of transportation networks, contributing to the overall development of communities. By efficiently collecting tolls, toll booth operators help sustain the quality and safety of roadways, which in turn aids economic activities, tourism, and connectivity. Their role extends beyond monetary transactions; they actively contribute to the functionality of modern transportation systems that underpin a thriving society.

Life as a toll booth operator comes with its own set of challenges. Operators often work in confined spaces, enduring long hours and exposure to varying weather conditions. The constant flow of vehicles demands keen attention to detail and the ability to handle stressful situations, such as handling impatient travelers and addressing technical glitches. Additionally, the advent of electronic toll collection systems has revolutionized the industry, shifting many toll transactions away from physical cash payments. Toll booth operators have had to adapt to these changes, becoming proficient in the operation of electronic tolling systems while continuing to provide excellent customer service.

Toll booth operators serve as the human face of transportation infrastructure, engaging with countless travelers on a daily basis. Their interactions range from brief exchanges of pleasantries to providing directions and assisting distressed travelers. Toll booth operators often witness the diverse tapestry of human experiences – from excited vacationers to weary commuters. They play a role in ensuring that the journey, even if interrupted by a toll, is pleasant and safe. These interactions not only reflect their professionalism but also contribute to the overall traveler experience.

The collection of tolls by operators is a cornerstone of transportation funding, providing a steady stream of revenue that supports maintenance, repairs, and expansion of infrastructure. These funds help reduce the burden on taxpayers while enabling the government to invest in new projects that enhance connectivity and accessibility. Toll booth operators, through their diligent work, play a direct role in ensuring that the financial resources required for the upkeep and development of transportation systems are readily available. In this way, their work contributes to the sustainable growth of both local and national economies.

Toll booth operators play an indirect yet crucial role in promoting road safety and efficiency. By ensuring that vehicles adhere to toll payment requirements, they contribute to the overall orderliness of traffic. The enforcement of toll collection regulations encourages compliance with traffic rules and regulations, which in turn reduces the likelihood of accidents and congestion. Their presence also aids in the prompt identification of any issues, such as malfunctioning toll systems or vehicles in need of assistance. Toll booth operators thus act as integral components of the broader effort to maintain road safety and traffic flow.

Toll booth operators may occupy seemingly small booths, but their impact on transportation infrastructure and society at large is substantial. They ensure the seamless flow of traffic, the funding of vital road maintenance projects, and the provision of a safe and pleasant traveler experience. While their work may often go unnoticed, it is an essential thread in the intricate fabric of modern transportation systems. As technology continues to evolve, toll booth operators adapt and embrace new methods of toll collection, remaining dedicated to their duty of facilitating the journey while contributing to the development and well-being of the communities they serve.

Harvesting Venom: Life as a Snake Milker and Venom Extractor

In the realm of unconventional professions that blur the lines between danger and fascination, one stands out – the snake milker. With a deft hand and an unyielding respect for the serpentine world, snake milkers extract potent venoms from some of the most venomous creatures on the planet. This daring occupation requires a unique combination of expertise, courage, and meticulous technique. In this section, we delve into the intriguing world of snake milkers, exploring the significance of their role, the perils they face, the intricate process of venom extraction, the applications of snake venom, and the crucial contribution of these professionals to science and medicine.

Snake milkers hold a role that intersects biology, medicine, and conservation. The venom extracted from snakes has a myriad of applications, ranging from the creation of antivenoms to scientific research and even potential medical breakthroughs. Venomous snake bites pose a significant health risk in various parts of the world, and snake milkers contribute to mitigating this risk by providing the essential raw material needed for antivenom production. Their work is vital for saving lives and advancing our understanding of these enigmatic creatures.

Being a snake milker involves navigating a realm of inherent danger. Dealing with venomous snakes carries an inherent risk, even for the most skilled professionals. Snake milkers must remain constantly vigilant and possess a deep understanding of snake behavior. A single mistake could lead to a potentially life-threatening bite. Their unwavering focus, steady hands, and ability to stay calm under pressure are the hallmarks of their bravery. These professionals acknowledge the danger, yet their commitment to their craft drives them to protect lives and advance scientific knowledge.

Venom extraction is an intricate and delicate process that requires both artistry and precision. Snake milkers use specialized techniques and tools to carefully coax the venom from the fangs of venomous snakes without harming the animal. The process involves the stimulation of the snake's venom glands, prompting the venom to flow into a collection container. This extracted venom is then carefully processed and preserved for various applications. The expertise required to handle venomous snakes, identify the right time for extraction, and execute the process safely reflects the high level of skill possessed by snake milkers.

Snake venom, once extracted, serves as a valuable resource in various fields. The creation of antivenoms, which are essential for treating snakebite victims, is perhaps the most crucial application. Additionally, snake venom contains a myriad of complex proteins and enzymes that have caught the attention of researchers in the fields of medicine and biology. Some of these compounds have shown potential in areas such as pain management, cancer research, and even treatment for neurological disorders. The applications of snake venom extend far beyond its feared reputation, revealing a treasure trove of potential medical breakthroughs.

Snake milkers are unsung heroes in the realms of science and medicine. Their work contributes to understanding the composition of venom, its effects on the body, and potential ways to harness its properties for therapeutic use. The production of antivenoms, developed from collected venom, is a lifeline for those at risk of snakebite. Additionally, their efforts contribute to our broader knowledge of snake species, behavior, and venom evolution. As scientific advancements continue, the work of snake milkers remains pivotal in unlocking the mysteries of these enigmatic creatures and translating their venom into life-saving solutions.

Snake milkers embody a blend of courage, expertise, and

dedication that sets them apart as unique and indispensable professionals. Their willingness to face danger in pursuit of advancing science, protecting lives, and unraveling the mysteries of venomous creatures is truly remarkable. By navigating the perilous realm of venomous snakes and extracting their potent elixir, snake milkers contribute to the development of antivenoms, scientific research, and potential medical breakthroughs. Their work underscores the intricate interplay between humans and the natural world, revealing that from the fangs of danger can emerge the promise of life-saving innovations.

Guardians of the Waters: The Vital Responsibility as a Lifeguard

Beside the shimmering waters of pools, lakes, and oceans, a silent sentinel stands watch—the lifeguard. This section delves into the profound responsibilities and challenges that define the life of a lifeguard, exploring their crucial role in safeguarding lives, the skills they master, the demands they face, the rewards they cherish, and the lasting impact they leave on those they protect.

Lifeguards are more than mere observers of aquatic activities; they are the guardians of safety in aquatic environments. Their primary duty is to prevent accidents and respond effectively to emergencies. Their presence ensures that swimmers and beachgoers can enjoy the water with a sense of security. With a watchful eye, they scan the waters, assess potential risks, and take swift action to prevent drowning and other water-related incidents. A lifeguard's role extends beyond rescue; it encompasses education, enforcing rules, and creating a culture of safety.

The role of a lifeguard demands a combination of physical skills, swift decision-making, and keen observational prowess. Lifeguards undergo rigorous training to master techniques such as CPR, first aid, and water rescue. They cultivate a deep understanding of aquatic environments, recognizing currents, waves, and potential hazards. Moreover, they develop exceptional communication skills to interact with diverse groups of people, from excited children to concerned parents. Their vigilance is unwavering, as they remain alert to signs of distress, swiftly responding to prevent emergencies from escalating.

Lifeguards confront a range of challenges, many of which stem from the unpredictable nature of water environments. They work long hours in varying weather conditions, often under the scorching sun or amidst turbulent waves. The responsibility to maintain concentration during slow periods and stay responsive when emergencies arise can be mentally taxing. Furthermore, lifeguards must remain fit and agile to execute physically demanding rescues. Balancing enforcement of safety rules with maintaining a friendly and approachable demeanor requires finesse. The emotional toll of dealing with life-threatening situations and potential loss can also be profound.

The rewards of being a lifeguard extend beyond a paycheck. Lifeguards find profound satisfaction in knowing that their vigilant presence can prevent tragedies and ensure that water activities remain enjoyable for everyone. Each rescue is a testament to their dedication, a life saved because of their swift action and well-honed skills. The gratitude expressed by those they've helped, the smiles of relieved parents, and the camaraderie formed with fellow lifeguards contribute to a sense of fulfillment that transcends the challenges.

The impact of lifeguards extends far beyond the immediate scope of their duty. Their dedication to safety fosters a culture of responsibility and awareness around water. Lifeguards often engage in educational initiatives, teaching individuals of all ages about water safety and drowning prevention. The lessons they impart empower people to make informed choices and be more cautious when enjoying aquatic activities. Additionally, the lifeguard's influence reaches into communities, inspiring young people to consider careers in public safety and promoting a heightened appreciation for the environment.

Lifeguards stand as the silent heroes who ensure that enjoyment and safety coexist at the water's edge. Their role transcends the confines of a job description; it's a commitment to saving lives, preventing accidents, and fostering a culture of responsibility. While the challenges they face can be daunting, the rewards they reap are immeasurable. Lifeguards exemplify the epitome of public service—dedicating themselves to the well-being of others, even in the face of uncertainty. Their legacy is woven into the fabric of aquatic safety, leaving an indelible mark on the lives they protect and the communities they serve. In a world where enjoyment meets potential danger, lifeguards stand unwaveringly as sentinels of safety, making the waters a place of joy and tranquility for all.

On the Road and In the Oven: Navigating Life as a Pizza Delivery Driver

In the world of fast food and convenience, the role of a pizza delivery driver may appear mundane at first glance. However, beneath the surface of speedy deliveries and hot boxes lies a dynamic profession that involves much more than just transporting pizzas. A pizza delivery driver bridges the gap between the pizzeria and the customer's doorstep, embodying punctuality, customer service, and adaptability. Beyond the practical aspects, this job offers a unique blend of challenges, interactions, and experiences that shape the daily life of those who embark on these delivery journeys. This section dives into the multifaceted world of pizza delivery driving, exploring the challenges, customer interactions, time management, and the sense of community that define this profession.

Pizza delivery drivers face a host of challenges on the road, from navigating unfamiliar neighborhoods to dealing with traffic congestion. These drivers must be adaptable and quick-witted, able to adjust their routes on the fly to ensure that piping hot pizzas reach their destination in a timely manner. Weather conditions, road closures, and other unexpected obstacles can further complicate the delivery process. The pressure to meet delivery times while ensuring food quality requires a delicate balance of speed and caution. Overcoming these challenges demands not only efficient driving skills but also the ability to maintain composure under pressure.

While the primary task of a pizza delivery driver is to deliver food, they also serve as the face of the pizzeria. Their interactions with customers are crucial in shaping the overall dining experience. A friendly smile, a courteous greeting, and efficient communication can go a long way in leaving a positive impression. Moreover, delivery drivers are often the ones to handle customer concerns, resolve issues, and ensure customer satisfaction. Their ability to manage customer expectations and resolve problems showcases their customer service skills, highlighting the pivotal role they play in the reputation of the pizzeria.

Efficiency is the cornerstone of successful pizza delivery. Drivers must manage multiple orders, optimize routes, and prioritize delivery times to ensure that customers receive their orders promptly. This aspect of time management is not just about delivering pizzas quickly; it's about maintaining a delicate balance between speed and safety. The pressure to meet delivery targets while adhering to traffic laws and ensuring food quality requires a high degree of organization. This ability to juggle various tasks while maintaining a focus on customer satisfaction showcases the resourcefulness and adaptability of pizza delivery drivers.

Pizza delivery drivers are often familiar faces in their delivery areas, which can lead to a unique sense of community. They become acquainted with regular customers, recognizing their preferences and building rapport over time. This connection between driver and customer transcends the transactional nature of the job, creating a small yet meaningful bond that contributes to the social fabric of the neighborhood. In addition, drivers often interact with employees of various establishments, from apartment buildings to offices, forging connections that extend beyond the pizza box. This sense of belonging and familiarity can enhance the overall job satisfaction for delivery drivers.

Pizza delivery drivers often work independently, spending a significant portion of their shifts alone on the road. This autonomy can be both liberating and challenging. On one hand, drivers enjoy a degree of freedom and flexibility, managing their routes and deliveries in a way that suits their preferences. On the other hand, this independence requires a strong sense of responsibility. Drivers must ensure the safe handling of food, accurate order delivery, and adherence to company policies. This blend of freedom and responsibility shapes the work ethic and personal growth of pizza delivery drivers, who learn to manage their tasks efficiently while maintaining a sense of accountability.

Being a pizza delivery driver is more than just delivering pizzas; it's about embracing challenges, serving customers with a smile, managing time and routes effectively, fostering community connections, and maintaining a balance between independence and responsibility. These drivers are the unsung heroes who ensure that hunger is quelled, taste buds are satisfied, and customers are left with positive impressions. Their role bridges the gap between the pizzeria and the customer's table, offering not only convenience but also a unique blend of experiences that shape their daily lives. In a world that values efficiency and service, pizza delivery drivers stand as ambassadors of both.

Stitching Dreams: The Artistry and Innovation of a Fashion Designer

Fashion designers, the visionaries behind clothing and style, hold a unique position in the world of art and commerce. With their creative flair, keen sense of aesthetics, and ability to capture cultural shifts, they shape the way we dress and express ourselves. This section explores into the realm of a fashion designer, exploring the significance of their role, the diverse responsibilities they shoulder, the skills they cultivate, the challenges they embrace, and the profound satisfaction that accompanies the transformation of fabric into wearable art.

Fashion designers are the storytellers of clothing, weaving narratives through fabric, form, and color. They influence culture, self-expression, and identity by designing pieces that reflect individualism and societal trends. Fashion designers contribute to the ever-evolving tapestry of style, redefining beauty standards, and challenging conventions. Beyond aesthetics, their creations have economic impact, shaping industries and influencing consumer behavior.

The responsibilities of a fashion designer span a wide spectrum, from conceiving designs to overseeing production. Designers start by identifying trends, drawing inspiration from art, history, culture, and personal experiences. They conceptualize designs, draft patterns, and select materials that bring their visions to life. Fashion designers collaborate with pattern makers, tailors, and production teams to ensure their designs are executed flawlessly. Additionally, they oversee fashion shows, marketing campaigns, and branding efforts to communicate their artistic vision to the world.

Being a successful fashion designer demands a fusion of artistic talent and technical expertise. Designers must have an acute sense of color, proportion, and composition to create visually compelling pieces. They also need a deep understanding of fabrics, textures, and garment construction techniques to ensure their designs are both wearable and comfortable. Proficiency in design software is crucial for translating ideas into digital formats. Moreover, communication skills are vital for collaborating with teams and conveying design concepts to clients and manufacturers.

The life of a fashion designer is not without its challenges. The industry is fiercely competitive, with designers vying for attention in an ever-changing landscape. The pressure to consistently innovate while staying true to one's aesthetic can be creatively demanding. Fashion designers often work long hours, especially during peak seasons, to meet deadlines and oversee production. Moreover, the unpredictable nature of consumer preferences and trends requires adaptability and resilience. However, the rewards are immense. The satisfaction of seeing one's designs worn by individuals, the thrill of unveiling a collection, and the opportunity to leave a lasting impact on culture and aesthetics make being a fashion designer a deeply gratifying career.

In conclusion, being a fashion designer is a dynamic voyage that marries artistic expression with business acumen. Fashion designers hold the power to shape how we present ourselves to the world, to reflect our moods, aspirations, and individuality through clothing. Their influence extends beyond runways; they are architects of cultural shifts, trendsetters, and storytellers. Despite the challenges, the rewards of seeing a sketch transformed into a wearable masterpiece, witnessing the resonance of one's creations in society, and leaving an indelible mark on the way people dress and perceive themselves make being a fashion designer a captivating and fulfilling path. Fashion designers are the custodians of beauty, embodying the confluence of artistry and innovation that defines the world of style.

Serving with Grace: A Waiter's Journey

The role of a waiter in the hospitality industry extends far beyond merely serving food and beverages. A skilled waiter is a pivotal element in creating a memorable dining experience for patrons. This section delves into the multifaceted world of being a waiter, exploring the significance of the role, the skills required, the challenges faced, the importance of customer service, and the potential for personal and professional growth within this profession.

Waitstaff are the face of a restaurant, representing its ambiance, cuisine, and service quality. A waiter's interactions with diners directly influence their perception of the establishment. The art of anticipating customers' needs, suggesting menu items, and ensuring a seamless dining experience is a delicate balancing act that elevates the dining journey from mere sustenance to a memorable event. A skilled waiter becomes a guide, enhancing the culinary adventure while fostering a sense of comfort and satisfaction.

Waitstaff excellence demands a unique set of skills. Beyond knowledge of the menu, waiters must possess exceptional communication, multitasking, and time management abilities. The ability to remain composed under pressure, handle difficult customers, and maintain an attentive demeanor is essential. Waiters also need to collaborate effectively with the kitchen staff, ensuring orders are accurate and timely. The physical demands of the job, including standing for long hours and carrying heavy trays, contribute to the challenge.

Exceptional customer service is at the heart of being a waiter. Each interaction presents an opportunity to create a positive impact, and skilled waitstaff can turn a simple meal into a memorable event. Attentiveness, active listening, and the ability to read cues from patrons are key components of exceptional service. A waiter's role extends beyond taking orders; it involves building rapport, offering recommendations, and ensuring that diners leave the restaurant with a sense of satisfaction that goes beyond the culinary.

While being a waiter may seem like a transient job, it offers significant potential for personal and professional growth. The hospitality industry provides a unique environment for honing interpersonal skills, adaptability, and problem-solving abilities. Waitstaff who exhibit excellence may be recognized and promoted to supervisory or managerial positions, offering opportunities to lead teams and contribute to the overall success of the restaurant. Additionally, the skills learned as a waiter, such as effective communication and conflict resolution, can be transferable to various other industries.

Being a waiter is a dynamic profession that requires a blend of technical skills, emotional intelligence, and a passion for creating delightful experiences. A waiter's role extends beyond delivering plates; it involves weaving together the threads of ambiance, service, and culinary offerings to craft a memorable dining narrative. With challenges ranging from demanding physical tasks to complex interactions, waitstaff who master the art of the profession can shine as pillars of hospitality. The potential for personal and professional growth, coupled with the satisfaction of contributing to memorable moments in people's lives, makes being a waiter not just a job, but a rewarding journey within the vibrant tapestry of the hospitality industry.

Journey of Deliveries: Life on the Road as a Mail Carrier

In an age of digital communication, the role of a mail carrier stands as a bridge between distant hearts and communities. Beyond its functional aspect, being a mail carrier encompasses a unique blend of responsibility, connection, and challenges. This section dives into the world of mail carriers, exploring the significance of their role, the skills required, the evolving landscape of postal services, the challenges they face, and the lasting impact they have on society.

Mail carriers hold a distinct place in society as the conduits of written communication and tangible connections. They serve as the bearers of news, cherished moments, and heartfelt sentiments, facilitating connections between individuals and communities. While the digital age has transformed communication, the tangible nature of letters and packages still holds a special place in our lives. Mail carriers play a vital role in preserving this tradition, ensuring that physical correspondence reaches its intended recipients.

Being a mail carrier requires a combination of physical stamina, organizational skills, and a commitment to customer service. Carriers must navigate complex routes, often on foot or in vehicles, to ensure timely and accurate deliveries. Organizational prowess is essential for managing packages, sorting mail, and maintaining an efficient delivery schedule. Exceptional customer service skills enable carriers to interact positively with the public, address inquiries, and build rapport within the community they serve.

The role of a mail carrier has evolved alongside advancements in technology. While traditional mail remains relevant, carriers now also handle the growing volume of online shopping deliveries. This shift has placed new demands on carriers, requiring adaptability in handling diverse packages and maintaining high standards of accuracy. As postal services integrate technology for tracking and efficient routing, carriers often find themselves as both traditional messengers and modern logistics professionals.

Mail carriers face a range of challenges in their daily tasks. Weather conditions, traffic congestion, and demanding delivery quotas can make the job physically demanding and mentally taxing. Navigating unfamiliar neighborhoods and addressing safety concerns further amplify the complexity. Despite these challenges, mail carriers demonstrate remarkable resilience. Their commitment to delivering the mail, rain or shine, reflects a dedication that often goes beyond the call of duty.

The work of a mail carrier extends beyond the delivery of letters and packages; it contributes to the fabric of society. Carriers are the unsung heroes who ensure that celebrations, condolences, and everyday correspondences reach their destinations. They foster connections between families, friends, and businesses, playing an integral role in strengthening communities. In an increasingly digital world, the tactile nature of mail remains a poignant reminder of our shared humanity. Thus, being a mail carrier is not just a job but a service that embodies connection, dedication, and the enduring power of personal communication.

Crafting Cocktails and
Connecting with Patrons

Bartending is not merely a profession; it is an art form that requires skill, creativity, and a keen understanding of human nature. Behind the bar counter, bartenders don't just mix drinks; they craft experiences and create connections with their patrons. This section delves into the multifaceted world of bartending, exploring the skills and qualities necessary for success, the art of mixology, the social aspects of the job, the challenges faced, and the enduring appeal of this unique profession.

To excel in the world of bartending, one must first acquire a diverse set of skills and qualities. Bartenders must possess an in-depth knowledge of the vast array of spirits, liqueurs, and mixers available, as well as an understanding of the art of mixology. The ability to balance flavors and create unique and tantalizing cocktails is central to their craft. Moreover, bartenders should be adept at multitasking, as they often handle multiple orders simultaneously, all while maintaining a friendly and engaging demeanor.

Customer service skills are paramount in this profession. A great bartender knows how to read their patrons, anticipate their needs, and provide a welcoming and enjoyable atmosphere. They are often therapists, confidants, and entertainers rolled into one. Patrons seek solace in the bartender's ear, share their joys and sorrows, and revel in the camaraderie of the bar. A bartender's ability to listen and empathize is as crucial as their ability to mix a perfect martini.

At the heart of bartending lies the art of mixology. Crafting cocktails is not just about pouring liquids into a glass; it is about creating a symphony of flavors that tantalize the taste buds and leave a lasting impression. A skilled bartender understands the science behind mixology, from the proper techniques for muddling, shaking, and stirring to the nuances of layering and garnishing.

Each cocktail is a work of art, with its own unique balance of ingredients. Whether it's a classic cocktail like the Old Fashioned or an innovative concoction designed to surprise and delight, bartenders approach their craft with a passion for experimentation. They are constantly exploring new ingredients and techniques to push the boundaries of flavor and presentation.

In addition to mastering the classics, bartenders often put their own spin on drinks, creating signature cocktails that reflect their personal style and the character of the establishment they work in. These creations become a source of pride and a way to leave a lasting mark on the industry.

Beyond the technical skills and creativity, bartending is fundamentally a social profession. Bartenders are the heart and soul of a bar, responsible for setting the tone and atmosphere. They are the gatekeepers of good times, facilitating connections between patrons and fostering a sense of community.

Bartenders often become confidants and friends to their regulars, offering a sympathetic ear and a warm smile. The bar counter becomes a place where people from all walks of life come together to celebrate, commiserate, and connect. In this sense, bartending transcends the act of serving drinks; it becomes a vehicle for building relationships and creating memories.

The social aspect of bartending also extends to the art of bartending competitions and industry events. Bartenders from around the world gather to showcase their skills, exchange ideas, and learn from one another. These events create a sense of camaraderie and mutual respect among those in the profession, reinforcing the idea that bartending is more than just a job; it's a lifestyle and a community.

Despite its many rewards, bartending comes with its fair share of challenges. The late hours and physically demanding nature of the job can take a toll on one's health and personal life. Dealing with difficult customers, managing intoxicated patrons, and navigating the complexities of alcohol-related laws and regulations are also part of the bartender's daily reality.

For those who are passionate about their craft, the rewards far outweigh the challenges. Bartending offers a unique opportunity for creativity, self-expression, and personal growth. It provides a platform for honing essential life skills, such as problem-solving, adaptability, and conflict resolution. The financial incentives, including tips and the potential for career advancement, make bartending an attractive choice for many. Furthermore, the intangible rewards of bartending are immeasurable. The satisfaction of creating a perfectly balanced cocktail, the joy of seeing patrons light up with delight, and the sense of belonging to a tight-knit community of like-minded individuals all contribute to the profound fulfillment that this profession can offer.

The enduring appeal of bartending lies in its ability to merge tradition with innovation, science with art, and service with social connection. It is a profession that thrives on the human need for interaction, celebration, and shared experiences. In an ever-evolving world, the role of the bartender remains a constant, providing a safe haven where people can unwind, socialize, and enjoy the pleasures of a well-crafted drink.

Bartending is more than a job; it is a vocation that requires a unique blend of skills, creativity, and social acumen. Bartenders are the architects of unforgettable experiences, the keepers of traditions, and the facilitators of connections. Despite its challenges, the enduring appeal of bartending lies in its ability to enrich the lives of both those who practice it and those who partake in the fruits of their labor. It is a profession that elevates the art of mixing drinks to the art of creating memories.

The Unsung Heroes of Cleanliness

In the backdrop of our bustling lives, there exists a group of dedicated individuals who often go unnoticed but play an indispensable role in maintaining our surroundings. Janitors, commonly referred to as custodians, perform the vital task of keeping our schools, workplaces, hospitals, and public spaces clean and safe. Let's explores the often-underappreciated profession of janitorial work, shedding light on the skills required, the importance of their role, the challenges they face, the unsung heroes who choose this path, and the profound impact they have on our daily lives.

The role of a janitor extends far beyond pushing a mop or wielding a broom. Janitors are the unsung heroes of cleanliness, responsible for maintaining the sanitation, hygiene, and overall appearance of various facilities. Their duties encompass a wide range of tasks, from sweeping and mopping floors to cleaning restrooms, emptying trash bins, and sanitizing surfaces. Janitors also perform essential maintenance work, such as changing light bulbs, fixing minor plumbing issues, and ensuring the safety of the premises by identifying potential hazards.

Janitors often work behind the scenes during non-business hours to minimize disruptions to daily operations. Their meticulous work ensures that when employees, students, or visitors arrive in the morning, they are greeted by a clean and orderly environment. The skill and dedication required for this profession cannot be underestimated, as janitors are entrusted with the responsibility of maintaining the health and well-being of the people who use these spaces.

Janitors are the silent observers of our lives, and their work often goes unnoticed until something is amiss. Despite the lack of recognition, they take immense pride in their work and are driven by a sense of duty and responsibility. Their unassuming demeanor belies the incredible impact they have on the overall quality of our lives.

These unsung heroes work diligently to ensure that our environments are not just clean but also safe. Their role in infection control, especially in healthcare facilities, cannot be overstated. During the COVID-19 pandemic, janitors played a crucial role in sanitizing and disinfecting public spaces, helping to slow the spread of the virus and protect the health of the community. In schools, janitors contribute to a conducive learning environment by maintaining classrooms, cafeterias, and playgrounds.

While janitors perform invaluable work, they face numerous challenges that can be physically demanding and emotionally taxing. The nature of the job often involves long hours, working evenings, nights, and weekends when buildings are empty. This can disrupt their work-life balance and make it challenging to spend time with their families.

The physical demands of the job can take a toll on janitors' health. Repetitive tasks, lifting heavy objects, and exposure to cleaning chemicals can lead to injuries and health issues over time. Moreover, janitors may face disrespect or indifference from some individuals who do not fully appreciate the importance of their work.

In addition to physical challenges, janitors often work in isolation, with limited interaction with the people they serve. This isolation can lead to feelings of loneliness and a lack of recognition for their efforts. Despite the challenges they face, janitors exhibit remarkable resilience and dedication. They take pride in their work, knowing that it directly contributes to the well-being and safety of others. Many janitors form strong bonds with the facilities they care for, viewing their work as a vital contribution to the community.

Janitors often display a sense of creativity and resourcefulness in problem-solving. They are skilled in using a variety of cleaning equipment and chemicals, and they adapt to the specific needs of each facility they serve. Their ability to handle unexpected situations, from spills and emergencies to equipment malfunctions, is a testament to their resourcefulness.

Janitors are the unsung heroes who work tirelessly to maintain the cleanliness and safety of our shared spaces. Their role is far more significant than meets the eye, encompassing a wide range of responsibilities that contribute to our overall quality of life. Janitors display unwavering dedication and resilience, overcoming physical and emotional challenges to perform their vital duties.

As we go about our daily lives, it is essential to recognize and appreciate the profound impact that janitors have on our well-being. Their work extends beyond cleaning; it ensures that our environments are conducive to productivity, learning, healing, and simply living. Janitors are the invisible hands that keep our world functioning smoothly, and they deserve our respect and gratitude for the vital role they play.

Thresholds of Success:
Navigating the World as a
Door-to-Door Salesperson

In an era dominated by digital marketing and e-commerce, the role of a door-to-door salesperson might seem archaic. However, this often-underestimated profession plays a pivotal role in building personal connections and fostering community engagement. Being a door-to-door salesperson is more than just selling products; it's about forging human connections, honing interpersonal skills, adapting to diverse environments, and mastering the art of resilience. This section adventures into the multifaceted world of door-to-door sales, exploring the challenges, rewards, and skills that define this profession.

At its core, being a door-to-door salesperson is about building meaningful connections with people. Unlike impersonal online interactions, face-to-face conversations provide a unique opportunity to understand individual needs, concerns, and aspirations. This personal touch creates a foundation of trust, enabling salespeople to tailor their pitches and recommendations to cater directly to the customer's situation. Whether selling educational products, home essentials, or renewable energy solutions, the salesperson becomes a bridge between the product and the customer's lifestyle. Each door opened is an invitation not just to sell, but to listen, empathize, and demonstrate the value a product can bring to the customer's life.

Being a successful door-to-door salesperson requires a high level of interpersonal skills. Effective communication, active listening, and the ability to read nonverbal cues are essential tools in the salesperson's arsenal. Salespeople must quickly adapt their communication style to suit the personality and preferences of each prospect. A warm smile, a confident handshake, and a genuine interest in the customer's needs can go a long way in establishing rapport. Moreover, the art of persuasion is refined through these interactions. Salespeople learn to present benefits in a compelling manner, address objections with empathy, and guide customers towards a decision that aligns with their best interests.

One of the most remarkable aspects of being a door-to-door salesperson is the exposure to diverse environments and communities. Every neighborhood has its own culture, socioeconomic status, and unique set of challenges. Adapting to these differences requires not only flexibility but also cultural sensitivity. A successful salesperson understands that a one-size-fits-all approach is ineffective. Instead, they learn to tailor their approach to each environment, showcasing products in a way that resonates with the specific needs and values of the community. This adaptability not only increases the chances of making a sale but also enriches the salesperson's understanding of human diversity.

The life of a door-to-door salesperson is not without its challenges. Enduring rejection, skepticism, and occasionally rude responses can be emotionally taxing. However, this environment cultivates a unique kind of resilience. Salespeople learn to handle rejection with grace, to not take negativity personally, and to maintain their enthusiasm despite adversity. Over time, this resilience extends beyond the professional realm, impacting personal growth and mindset. The ability to stay positive in the face of rejection, coupled with the determination to persevere, is a testament to the strong character forged through the trials of the job.

In an era where technology often mediates our interactions, the role of a door-to-door salesperson stands as a testament to the enduring power of face-to-face communication. This profession is a bridge that spans physical thresholds and connects individuals on a personal level.

Through building connections, mastering interpersonal skills, adapting to diverse environments, and cultivating resilience, door-to-door salespeople contribute not only to the economy but also to the social fabric of communities. Their journeys are a testament to the art of persuasion, the value of human connection, and the resilience of the human spirit.

Driving Dreams: The Art
of Car Salesmanship

Car salespersons, the interface between customers and the automotive industry, play a pivotal role in helping individuals find their ideal vehicles. With a mix of product knowledge, interpersonal skills, and a deep understanding of customer needs, they facilitate the process of purchasing cars. This section delves into the realm of a car salesperson, exploring the significance of their role, the diverse responsibilities they shoulder, the skills they cultivate, the challenges they face, and the sense of satisfaction that comes from connecting customers with their dream vehicles.

Car salespersons are instrumental in bridging the gap between car manufacturers and buyers. Their role extends beyond merely selling vehicles; they provide guidance, information, and reassurance to customers making a significant investment. They assist customers in finding vehicles that align with their preferences, budget, and lifestyle. In doing so, car salespersons become enablers of mobility and a crucial link in the automotive industry's value chain.

The responsibilities of a car salesperson encompass an array of roles, all centered around delivering an exceptional customer experience. They listen attentively to customers' preferences and requirements, providing knowledgeable insights into different vehicle models, features, and specifications. Car salespersons often facilitate test drives, allowing customers to experience firsthand the vehicles they are considering. They handle negotiations, ensuring transparency and fairness in pricing. Moreover, they manage administrative tasks related to paperwork, financing, and vehicle delivery, streamlining the entire purchasing process.

Being a successful car salesperson requires a blend of technical knowledge, communication skills, and customer-centricity. A deep understanding of automotive technology and features allows salespersons to provide accurate and relevant information to customers. Effective communication and interpersonal skills enable them to build rapport, listen to customer preferences, and address any concerns. Negotiation skills are vital for finding common ground on pricing and terms. Additionally, staying updated on industry trends, market dynamics, and financing options is crucial for offering well-informed recommendations.

The life of a car salesperson comes with its own set of challenges. The sales process can be competitive, requiring persistence and resilience to handle rejections and navigate negotiations. Meeting sales targets and quotas can be stressful, and the fluctuating nature of the market can impact business. Building trust with customers and managing their expectations demands emotional intelligence and professionalism. However, the rewards are significant. The satisfaction of matching customers with vehicles that suit their needs, witnessing the joy of a successful purchase, and earning commissions based on one's efforts are among the many gratifying aspects of the profession.

In conclusion, being a car salesperson is a multifaceted role that merges product knowledge, interpersonal skills, and customer service excellence. Salespersons serve as the bridge between customers' desires and the automotive industry's offerings, guiding individuals through the process of purchasing vehicles. Beyond selling cars, they foster relationships built on trust and understanding. Despite the challenges, the rewards of facilitating mobility, connecting customers with their dream vehicles, and contributing to the automotive industry's success make being a car salesperson a fulfilling endeavor. Salespersons stand at the forefront of the customer experience, shaping the perception of brands and creating memorable journeys for those seeking to drive their dreams.

Serving with Honor: Embarking on a Career in the Military

A career in the military is a path of unwavering dedication, sacrifice, and service to one's nation. Those who choose this calling embark on a journey that demands courage, resilience, and a profound commitment to safeguarding freedom and security. This section dives into the world of a military career, exploring the significance of this path, the diverse roles and responsibilities it entails, the unique skills it cultivates, the challenges it presents, and the indomitable sense of purpose that accompanies those who serve in uniform.

A military career is a call to defend, protect, and uphold the ideals that a nation holds dear. Military personnel are the guardians of national sovereignty, standing as a bulwark against threats both internal and external. They play an instrumental role in maintaining peace and stability, responding to emergencies, and providing humanitarian aid. The essence of a military career lies in the commitment to safeguarding the values and freedoms that a society cherishes, often at great personal sacrifice.

A military career encompasses a spectrum of roles that extend far beyond combat. Military personnel serve as defenders, strategists, engineers, medical professionals, and peacekeepers. They are responsible for national defense, intelligence gathering, disaster relief, and international cooperation. While some serve on the front lines, others work behind the scenes to ensure logistics, communication, and intelligence operations run seamlessly. These diverse roles reflect the multifaceted nature of a military career, where each individual contributes to a greater collective purpose.

A military career imparts a unique set of skills that extend beyond military tactics. Leadership skills are nurtured from day one, as personnel are tasked with making split-second decisions that can impact lives. Discipline is instilled through rigorous training that demands adherence to protocols and standards. Teamwork and camaraderie are fostered through shared experiences and the understanding that each individual plays an integral role. Adaptability and resilience are honed in the face of unpredictable and challenging situations.

A military career is marked by both challenges and rewards. The demands of training, deployments, and prolonged separations from family and loved ones can be emotionally and physically taxing. The exposure to danger and the potential for trauma are inherent risks. Yet, the rewards are deeply meaningful. The honor of serving one's country, the opportunity to make a tangible difference, and the bonds formed with fellow servicemembers create a sense of camaraderie that is unparalleled. Moreover, the training and skills acquired during a military career often translate seamlessly into civilian life, providing a solid foundation for future endeavors.

In conclusion, a career in the military is a noble path that calls for selflessness, dedication, and an unwavering commitment to the greater good. Those who choose this journey embrace challenges with courage, exemplify discipline and honor, and embody the principles that a nation stands for. The significance of a military career lies in the protection of cherished values, the preservation of peace, and the resilience to face adversity head-on. Despite the hardships, the rewards of serving one's country, the opportunity to make a lasting impact, and the privilege of being part of a legacy of valor make a military career an exceptional and deeply meaningful choice. Military personnel stand as beacons of bravery, embodying the essence of service and sacrifice.

Empowering Change
Through Philanthropy

Philanthropy is the embodiment of compassion and generosity in action. A philanthropist, driven by a desire to create positive change, dedicates time, resources, and influence to support various charitable causes. Let's travel into the world of philanthropy, exploring the motivations behind becoming a philanthropist, the various forms of philanthropic giving, the impact it has on society, the challenges faced, and the profound satisfaction that comes from giving back to the community.

At the core of philanthropy lies the unwavering desire to make the world a better place. Philanthropists are individuals who have been blessed with resources and privilege and have made a conscious choice to use these advantages for the greater good. Their motivations vary, ranging from personal experiences to a sense of moral duty or a desire to leave a lasting legacy.

Philanthropy is not merely a financial endeavor; it is an emotional and deeply personal commitment to addressing pressing issues, such as poverty, education, healthcare, environmental conservation, and social justice. Philanthropists are often guided by a strong sense of empathy and a belief in the power of collective action to effect positive change. They view their wealth and influence as tools for creating a more equitable and compassionate world.

Philanthropic giving takes on various forms, each tailored to the philanthropist's individual preferences and the causes they are passionate about. Financial donations are a common avenue for giving, with philanthropists contributing significant sums to nonprofit organizations, charities, and foundations. These funds may be used for a wide range of purposes, from supporting research and development to funding educational scholarships or providing relief in times of crisis.

Beyond financial donations, philanthropists often offer their expertise, time, and networks to amplify the impact of their giving. They may serve on the boards of nonprofit organizations, offer mentorship to individuals in need, or leverage their influence to raise awareness and mobilize resources for a particular cause. In essence, philanthropy is a holistic commitment that extends beyond financial support to encompass active engagement and advocacy.

The impact of philanthropy on society is immeasurable. Philanthropists have played a pivotal role in addressing some of the world's most pressing challenges. Their contributions have fueled groundbreaking medical research, expanded access to education, provided relief in times of natural disasters, and empowered marginalized communities. Philanthropic initiatives often serve as catalysts for broader social change. For example, philanthropists who invest in educational programs can help break the cycle of poverty by providing opportunities for underprivileged youth. Similarly, those dedicated to environmental causes can drive innovation and awareness, leading to more sustainable practices on a global scale.

Philanthropy also has a ripple effect, inspiring others to join in the cause. When high-profile philanthropists champion a particular issue, they can mobilize public support and encourage additional contributions from individuals, corporations, and governments. This amplification of resources and attention is a testament to the far-reaching influence of philanthropy. Despite the noble intentions of philanthropy, it is not without its challenges. Philanthropists often grapple with complex decisions regarding where and how to allocate their resources. Determining which causes to support, evaluating the impact of their donations, and ensuring that funds are used effectively can be daunting tasks.

Philanthropy can sometimes be met with skepticism

or criticism. Questions about transparency, accountability, and the potential for undue influence may arise. Philanthropists must navigate these concerns with transparency and ethical practices to maintain public trust and ensure that their efforts have a positive impact. The enormity of the world's problems can be overwhelming, and philanthropists may feel the weight of responsibility to address multiple issues simultaneously. Balancing personal, professional, and philanthropic commitments can be a significant challenge.

In spite of the challenges, the satisfaction that comes from philanthropy is profound. Philanthropists experience a deep sense of fulfillment knowing that their actions are making a tangible difference in the lives of others and in the world at large. They witness the transformation of communities, the advancement of knowledge, and the alleviation of suffering resulting from their generosity. Philanthropy allows individuals to connect with like-minded people who share their passion for making a positive impact. This sense of community and shared purpose can be deeply rewarding, fostering a sense of belonging and camaraderie among philanthropists and the organizations they support.

Philanthropy is a testament to the capacity for compassion and generosity that resides within individuals. Philanthropists, driven by a desire to create positive change, play a pivotal role in addressing some of the world's most pressing challenges. Their commitment to giving back, in various forms, has a profound and lasting impact on society. While philanthropy comes with its challenges, the deep satisfaction and sense of purpose that it brings to the lives of philanthropists make it a profoundly rewarding journey. It underscores the enduring belief that, by working together, we can build a better, more compassionate world for all.

Conclusion

In the pages of this book, we have embarked on a journey through the vast landscape of career possibilities, each chapter unveiling a new facet of the intricate mosaic that shapes our professional world. In the tapestry of life's journey, the myriad paths we tread weave a rich and diverse narrative that defines the human experience. This book has aimed to illuminate the spectrum of career paths available to us, showcasing the kaleidoscope of passions, talents, and aspirations that drive individuals toward unique vocations. As we conclude this exploration, we are reminded that the tapestry of careers is as diverse and dynamic as the individuals who pursue them. As we close this book, we are reminded that every path, whether conventional or unconventional, contributes to the collective tapestry that forms our society.

Each story shared within these pages is a testament to the power of choice, the pursuit of dreams, and the triumph of resilience. From the towering achievements of renowned scientists to the quiet dedication of caregivers, we have encountered stories of passion, determination, and the unyielding pursuit of excellence. These narratives underscore the human spirit's capacity to transcend challenges and embrace opportunities, no matter the chosen path. Whether navigating the complexities of business, the realms of artistry, the frontlines of healthcare, or the uncharted territories of innovation, every career path leaves an indelible mark on our collective journey.

Throughout these chapters, a common thread of resilience and adaptability has emerged. As individuals forge their own paths, they navigate unexpected turns, celebrate triumphs, and learn from setbacks. This resilience is a testament to the power of human potential and the innate drive to excel, to contribute, and to leave a lasting impact on the world around us.

As we close this book, let us carry forward the wisdom gained from these diverse stories. Let us recognize that there is no single "right" path to success, but rather a multitude of avenues waiting to be explored. The mosaic of careers reflects the beautiful complexity of our aspirations, and each thread woven into this tapestry enhances its vibrancy. As we turn the final page, let us carry forward the wisdom gleaned from these stories. Let us embrace the idea that the journey of discovering one's path is not linear – it's an exploration that evolves over time, influenced by experiences, insights, and the relentless pursuit of growth. May this book inspire readers to approach their own paths with a spirit of curiosity, resilience, and an unwavering belief in their unique abilities.

In a world brimming with possibilities, may this book serve as a reminder that our career choices are not just means to a livelihood, but pathways to personal fulfillment, societal progress, and the realization of dreams. Let us remember that no matter the path we choose, we are all contributing to this intricate and magnificent tapestry, leaving an indelible mark on the legacy of generations to come. As we navigate our own journeys, may we draw inspiration from the stories shared within these pages and forge ahead with determination, purpose, and a sense of boundless opportunity. Our lives are the canvas upon which we paint our unique stories, and in doing so, we contribute to the ever-evolving narrative of human achievement and aspiration.